THE PENGUIN POETS

D19

COMIC AND CURIOUS

VERSE

The Penguin Book of

COMIC AND CURIOUS

VERSE

∽

COLLECTED BY

J. M. Cohen

PENGUIN BOOKS

Penguin Books Ltd, Harmondsworth, Middlesex
AUSTRALIA: Penguin Books Pty Ltd, 762 Whitehorse Road,
Mitcham, Victoria

—

First published 1952
Reprinted 1952, 1954, 1956, 1958

Made and printed in Great Britain
by The Whitefriars Press Ltd
London and Tonbridge

To the Memory of

MY FATHER

*who first introduced me to
the Ingoldsby Legends
and to*

MY FOUR SONS

*to whom in turn I have
introduced some of my
favourite poets*

∾

Contents

Foreword

THE territory of the 'Comic and Curious' does not lend itself to easy definition. Somewhere between 'The Dunciad' and Edgell Rickword's 'Encounter' lies the frontier dividing the strict kingdom of satire from the more boisterous and anarchic republic of comic expostulation. Somewhere again between 'Hans Carvel' and 'Tam O' Shanter' falls the border where humorous distortion gives place to ironic narrative. Somewhere, too, on the hither side of de la Mare's 'Peacock Pie' there is a line separating the comic and whimsical from pure fantasy. I will freely confess that I have made several raids into the marches beyond the strict frontiers of the 'Comic and Curious'; but the justification for my forays lies in the rich booty that I have brought back. I cannot think that any readers would have wished me to forego the description of Philip Sparrow's funeral, 'Three Young Rats' or James Michie's brilliant but unclassifiable 'Arizona Nature Myth', all of which I must admit to have snatched from the borderlands. Like any good anthologist, I have indulged my personal tastes, in particular a weakness for fantastic portraiture. But I am confident that I have not let my own preferences crowd out good things which might have stronger claims to my attention, and that I have chosen many pieces which will be unfamiliar to all my readers, many that will make them laugh, many that will draw a smile, and many that will raise a round of silent applause for their wit, their accomplishment or their mere 'curiousness'.

I have limited myself, but for my inclusion of Skelton, almost entirely to the last three centuries. In earlier poems the point of the joke is too often obscured by the language or even by the style of humour. I have combed the seventeenth-century miscellanies and found quite a few pieces that deserve to be put back into circulation, and similar explorations of eighteenth-century collections have been even more fruitful. The book, of course, contains many of the old favourites. It would be absurd to exclude anything by Lewis Carroll, Lear or W. S. Gilbert merely because it is familiar. I have, however, drawn much more freely on Prior and Thomas Hood than anthologists have done before me. Both are unduly neglected, Hood in particular. For his ingenuity and his tremendous mastery of language and metre fail to show up in those punning poems of his – entertaining though they are – by which he is usually represented.

The book's division into eight sections: 'Birds, Beasts, and Humans', 'Unlikely Stories', 'For Various Occasions', 'Protests and Expostulations', 'Rigmaroles and Nonsense', 'Whims and Oddities', 'Burlesque and Parody', and 'Street Corner Songs', is an arbitrary one. Many of the pieces could conveniently be included under any one of two or three headings. Indeed, the epigrams, epitaphs, lampoons and limericks which I have chosen to fill up the odd spaces cannot be said to belong to any of the eight sections at all. But this arrangement seems to me more pleasant and informal than a strictly chronological one.

I owe very considerable debts to my predecessors – to Mr W. H. Beable for his collection of Epitaphs, and to such general anthologies as Sir John Squire's *Comic Muse*, Michael Roberts' *Faber Book of Modern Verse*, W. H. Auden's *Oxford Book of Light Verse*, Auden and Garrett's *The Poet's Tongue*, *The Week-End Book*, and to a collection by Carolyn Wells published in the U.S.A. Sometimes I have taken from one or another of them a poem that I had not found at source; sometimes they have guided me to a book or an author whom otherwise I should have missed. I have followed Michael Roberts in one or two particulars, among them in his ruthless compression of Southey's 'March to Moscow', while to Auden I owe 'Charlie Piecan', which had not been printed before he pieced together his version for the *Oxford Book*. To him also I owe 'The Common Cormorant', which I have always suspected to be a composition of his own fathered by him on that broad-shouldered old reprobate, Anon.

Others who have helped in the compilation of this book by generously offering suggestions include John Betjeman, C. J. Greenwood, John Dobell, John Gloag, Derek Hudson, and Edward Upward. To each of them I owe inclusions that without them I should never have found.   J.M.C.

Acknowledgements

FOR permission to reprint copyright matter the following acknowledgements are made:

For poems by W. H. Auden to the author and Messrs Faber & Faber Ltd, *Another Time* and *New Year Letter* (Faber); for poems by Hilaire Belloc to the author and Messrs Gerald Duckworth & Co. Ltd, *Sonnets and Verse* (Duckworth), *Cautionary Verses* (Duckworth); for poems by John Betjeman to the author and Messrs John Murray, *Selected Poems* (Murray); for poems by Morris Bishop to the author and G. P. Putnam & Sons; for poems by G. K. Chesterton to the author's executrix, Messrs A. P. Watt and Messrs Methuen & Co. Ltd, *Collected Poems of G. K. Chesterton* (Methuen); for poems by E. E. Cummings to the author and Harcourt Brace & Co. Ltd; for poems by Walter de la Mare to the author and Messrs Faber & Faber Ltd, *Collected Rhymes and Verses* (Faber); for a poem by Lawrence Durrell to the author and Messrs Faber & Faber Ltd, *Cities, Plains and People* (Faber); for a poem by T. S. Eliot to the author and Messrs Faber & Faber Ltd, *Old Possum's Book of Practical Cats* (Faber); for poems by Sir W. S. Gilbert to Miss Nancy McIntosh and to Macmillan & Co. Ltd, *Bab Ballads* (Macmillan), *Savoy Operas* (Macmillan); for a poem by John Gloag to the author, A. D. Peters and Messrs George Allen & Unwin Ltd, *Board Room Ballads* (Allen & Unwin); for a poem by A. D. Godley to his executors and The Oxford University Press, *Fifty Poems by A. D. Godley* (Oxford); for poems by Harry Graham to Mrs Graham, Messrs A. P. Watt & Son, Edward Arnold Ltd, and Messrs Mills & Boon, *Departmental Ditties* (Mills & Boon), *Ruthless Rhymes* (Arnold); for poems by Robert Graves to the author, *Collected Poems 1914–26* (Heinemann) and *Poems and Satires 1951* (Cassell); for a poem by W. E. Henley to the poet's executor and Messrs Macmillan & Co. Ltd, *Poems by W. E. Henley* (Macmillan); for poems by Samuel Hoffenstein to the author and the Liveright Publishing Corporation; for a poem by A. E. Housman to the Society of Authors, as the Literary Representative of the trustees of the author's estate and Messrs Jonathan Cape Ltd; for poems by D. H. Lawrence to Mrs Frieda Lawrence, *Collected Poems* (Heinemann); for a poem by C. G. Leland to Messrs Routledge & Kegan Paul Ltd; for a poem by Archibald MacLeish to the poet and Messrs John Lane (The Bodley Head) Ltd, *Poems by Archibald MacLeish* (Lane); for poems by Don Marquis to Mrs Marquis and to Faber & Faber Ltd; for poems by Ewart Milne to the poet and Messrs John Lane (The Bodley Head) Ltd, *Diamond Cut Diamond* (Lane); for poems by Ogden Nash to the author, Messrs Curtis Brown and J. M. Dent & Sons Ltd; for a poem by John Pudney to the author and Messrs John Lane (The Bodley Head) Ltd, *Low Life* (Lane); for poems by Edgell Rickword to the author and Messrs John Lane (The Bodley Head) Ltd, *Collected Poems of Edgell Rickword* (Lane); for a poem by E. V. Rieu to the author and Messrs Methuen, *Cuckoo Calling* (Methuen); for a poem by Sir Owen Seaman and three limericks from *Mr Punch's Limerick Book* to the proprietors of *Punch;* for poems by Dr Edith Sitwell to the author and Messrs Pearn, Pollinger & Higham Ltd, Messrs Gerald Duckworth & Co. Ltd, and Messrs Macmillan & Co. Ltd; for poems by Sir Osbert Sitwell to the author, Messrs Pearn, Pollinger & Higham Ltd and Messrs Gerald Duckworth & Co. Ltd; for permission to use Philip Henderson's edition of John Skelton to Messrs J. M. Dent & Sons Ltd, *Complete Poems of John Skelton* (Dent); for a poem by James Stephens to the author's executors and Messrs Macmillan & Co. Ltd, *Collected Poems by James Stephens* (Macmillan); for a poem by A. C. Swinburne to the author's executors and William Heinemann & Co. Ltd, *Collected Poetical Works* (Heinemann); for poems by the Rev. L. Sandys Wason to Mrs Poore, his executrix; and to the following authors for various of their poems: E. C. Bentley, Norman Cameron, Gavin Ewart, Robert Lowry, Hughes Mearns, James Michie, William Plomer, Sir John Squire, and Geoffrey Taylor; and to the owners of Arnold Bennett's copyrights for a limerick by him.

BIRDS, BEASTS, AND
HUMANS

❧

Then Margery Milkduck
Her kirtle she did uptuck
An inch above her knee
Her legs that ye might see;
But they were sturdy and stubbéd,
Mighty pestles and clubbéd,
As fair and as white
As the foot of a kite:
She was somewhat foul,
Crooked-necked like an owl;
And yet she brought her fees,
A cantel of Essex cheese,
Was well a foot thick
Full of maggots quick:
It was huge and great,
And mighty strong meat
For the devil to eat
It was tart and pungete![1]

Another set of sluts:
Some brought walnuts,
Some apples, some pears,
Some brought their clipping shears,
Some brought this and that,
Some brought I wot n'ere what;
Some brought their husband's hat,
Some puddings and links,
Some tripes that stinks.
But of all this throng
One came them among,
She seemed half a leech,
And began to preach

1. pungent.

Of the Tuesday in the week
When the mare doth kick,
Of the virtue of an unset leek,
Of her husband's breek;
With the feathers of a quail
She could to Bordeaux sail;
And with good ale barmè
She could make a charmè
To help withal a stitch:
She seemed to be a witch.

Another brought two goslings
That were naughty froslings [1];
She brought them in a wallet,
She was a comely callet [2]:
The goslings were untied,
Elinor began to chide,
'They be wretchocks [3] thou hast brought,
They are sheer shaking nought!'

JOHN SKELTON

On Otho

Three daughters Otho hath, his onely heirs,
But will by no means let them learn to write;
'Cause, after his own humour much he fears,
They'll one day learn, love-letters to indite.
The youngest now's with childe; who taught her then,
Or of her self learn'd she to hold her pen?

ANON.

1. worthless frostbitten things.   2. jade.   3. the smallest of the brood.

How the First Hielandman was Made

God and Saint Peter was gangand be the way
Heich up in Argyll where their gait lay.
Saint Peter said to God, in ane sport word –
'Can ye nocht mak a Hielandman of this horse turd?'
God turned owre the horse turd with his pykit staff,
And up start a Hielandman black as ony draff.
Quod God to the Hielandman, 'Where wilt thou now?'
'I will doun in the Lawland, Lord, and there steal a cow.'
'And thou steal a cow, carle, there they will hang thee.'
'What reck, Lord, of that, for anis mon I die.'
God then he leuch and owre the dyke lap,
And out of his sheath his gully outgat.
Saint Peter socht the gully fast up and doun,
Yet could not find it in all that braid roun.
'Now,' quod God, 'here a marvell, how can this be,
That I suld want my gully, and we here bot three.'
'Humf,' quod the Hielandman, and turned him about,
And at his plaid neuk the gully fell out.
'Fy,' quod Saint Peter, 'thou will never do weill;
And thou bot new made and sa soon gais to steal.'
'Humf,' quod the Hielandman, and sware be yon kirk,
'Sa lang as I may gear get to steal, I will never wirk.'

ANON.

On a German Tour

I went to Strasburg, where I got drunk
With that most learn'd Professor Brunk:
I went to Wortz, where I got drunken
With that more learn'd Professor Ruhnken.

RICHARD PORSON

Sir Hudibras, His Passing Worth

He was in *Logick* a great Critick,
Profoundly skill'd in Analytick.
He could distinguish, and divide
A Hair 'twixt *South* and *South-West* side:
On either which he would dispute,
Confute, change hands, and still confute.
He'd undertake to prove by force
Of Argument, a Man's no Horse.
He'd prove a Buzard is no Fowl,
And that a *Lord* may be an Owl;
A Calf an *Alderman*, a Goose a *Justice*,
And Rooks *Committee-men* and *Trustees.*
He'd run in Debt by Disputation,
And pay with Ratiocination,
All this by Syllogism, true
In Mood and Figure, he would do.

In *Mathematicks* he was greater
Than *Tycho Brahe*, or *Erra Pater:*
For he by *Geometrick* scale
Could take the size of *Pots of Ale;*
Resolve by Signes and Tangents straight,
If *Bread* or *Butter* wanted weight;
And wisely tell what hour o'th day
The Clock does strike, by *Algebra*.

Beside he was a shrewd *Philosopher;*
And had read every Text and gloss over:
What e'er the crabbed'st Author hath
He understood b'implicit Faith,
What ever *Sceptick* could inquere for;
For every *why* he had a *wherefore:*
Knew more then forty of them do,

As far as words and terms could go.
All which he understood by Rote,
And as occasion serv'd, would quote;
No matter whether right or wrong:
They might be either said or sung.
His Notions fitted things so well,
That which was which he could not tell;
But oftentimes mistook the one
For th'other, as Great Clerks have done.
He could reduce all things to Acts
And knew their Natures by Abstracts,
Where Entity and Quiddity
The Ghosts of defunct Bodies flie;
Where Truth in Person does appear,
Like words congeal'd in Northern Air.
He knew *what's what*, and that's as high
As *Metaphysick* wit can fly.
In *School Divinity* as able
As he that hight *Irrefragable;*
Profound in all the Nominal
And real ways beyond them all,
And with as delicate a Hand
Could twist as tough a Rope of Sand,
And weave fine Cobwebs, fit for skull
That's empty when the moon is full;
Such as take Lodgings in a Head
That's to be lett unfurnished.
He could raise Scruples dark and nice,
And after solve 'em in a trice:
As if Divinity had catch'd
The Itch, of purpose to be scratch'd;
Or, like a Mountebank, did wound
And stab herself with doubts profound,
Only to shew with how small pain
The sores of faith are cur'd again;
Although by woful proof we find,

They always leave a Scar behind.
He knew the Seat of Paradise,
Could tell in what degree it lies:
And, as he was dispos'd, could prove it,
Below the Moon, or else above it:
What *Adam* dreamt of when his Bride
Came from her Closet in his side:
Whether the Devil tempted her
By a *High Dutch* Interpreter:
If either of them had a Navel;
Who first made Musick malleable:
Whether the Serpent at the fall
Had cloven Feet, or none at all,
All this without a Gloss or Comment,
He would unriddle in a moment
In proper terms, such as men smatter
When they throw out and miss the matter.

SAMUEL BUTLER

Hypocrisy

Hypocrisy will serve as well
To propagate a church as zeal;
As persecution and promotion
Do equally advance devotion:
So round white stones will serve, they say,
As well as eggs to make hens lay.

SAMUEL BUTLER

The China-Mender

Good morning, Mr What-d'ye-call! Well, here's another pretty
    job!
Lord help my Lady! – what a smash! if you had only heard her sob!
It was all through Mr Lambert: but for certain he was winy,
To think for to go to sit down in a table full of Chiny.
'Deuce take your stupid head!' says my Lady to his very face;
But politeness, you know, is nothing, when there's Chiny in the
    case:
And if ever a woman was fond of Chiny to a passion
It's my mistress, and all sorts of it, whether new or old fashion.
Her brother's a sea-captain, and brings her home ship-loads –
Such bronzes, and such dragons, and nasty, squatting things like
    toads;
And great nidnoddin mandarins, with palsies in the head:
I declare I've often dreamt of them, and had nightmares in my bed.
But the frightfuller they are – lawk! she loves them all the better:
She'd have Old Nick himself made of Chiny if they'd let her.
Lawk-a-mercy! break her Chiny, and it's breaking her very heart;
If I touch'd it, she would very soon say, 'Mary, we must part.'
To be sure she is unlucky: only Friday comes Master Randall,
And breaks a broken spout, and fresh chips a tea-cup handle:
He's a dear, sweet little child, but he will so finger and touch,
And that's why my Lady doesn't take to children much.
Well! there's stupid Mr Lambert, with his two great coat flaps,
Must go and sit down on the Dresden shepherdess's laps,
As if there was no such things as rosewood chairs in the room;
I couldn't have made a greater sweep with the handle of the broom.
Mercy on us! how my mistress began to rave and tear!
Well! after all, there's nothing like good ironstone ware for wear.
If ever I marry, that's flat, I'm sure it wont be John Dockery,
I should be a wretched woman in a shop full of crockery.
I should never like to wipe it, though I love to be neat and tidy,
And afraid of mad bulls on market-days every Monday and Friday.

I'm very much mistook if Mr Lambert's will be a catch;
The breaking the Chiny will be the breaking off of his own match.
Missis wouldn't have an angel, if he was careless about Chiny;
She never forgives a chip, if it's ever so small and tiny,
Lawk! I never saw a man in all my life in such a taking;
I could find in my heart to pity him for all his mischief-making.
To see him stand a-hammering and stammering, like a zany;
But what signifies apologies, if they won't mend old Chaney!
If he sent her up whole crates full, from Wedgwood's and Mr
    Spode's,
He couldn't make amends for the cracked mandarins and smash'd
    toads.
Well! every one has their tastes, but, for my parts, my own self,
I'd rather have the figures on my poor dear grandmother's old
    shelf:
A nice pea-green poll-parrot, and two reapers with brown ears of
    corns,
And a shepherd with a crook after a lamb with two gilt horns,
And such a Jemmy Jessamy in top-boots and sky-blue vest,
And a frill and flowered waistcoat, with a fine bowpot at the breast.
God help her, poor old soul! I shall come into 'em at her death,
Though she's a hearty woman for her years, except her shortness of
    breath.
Well! you think the things will mend — if they wont, Lord mend us
    all!
My Lady will go in fits, and Mr Lambert wont need to call:
I'll be bound in any money, if I had a guinea to give,
He wont sit down again on Chiny the longest day he has to live.
Poor soul! I only hope it wont forbid his banns of marriage,
Or he'd better have sat behind on the spikes of my Lady's carriage.
But you'll join 'em all of course, and stand poor Mr Lambert's
    friend;
I'll look in twice a day, just to see, like, how they mend.
To be sure it is a sight that might draw tears from dogs and cats;
Here's this pretty little pagoda, now, has lost four of its cocked
    hats:

Be particular with the pagoda: and then here's this pretty bowl! –
The Chinese Prince is making love to nothing because of this hole;
And here's another Chinese man, with a face just like a doll –
Do stick his pigtail on again, and just mend his parasol.
But I needn't tell you what to do; only do it out of hand,
And charge whatever you like to charge – my Lady won't make a
          stand.
Well! good morning, Mr What-d'ye-call; for it's time our gossip
          ended:
And you know the proverb, the less as is said, the sooner the
          Chiny's mended.

THOMAS HOOD

Dr Douglas's Marriage with Miss Mainwaring

St Paul has declared that persons though twain,
In marriage united one flesh shall remain:
But had he been by when, like Pharaoh's kind pairing,
Dr Douglas of Bene't espoused Miss Mainwaring,
The Apostle no doubt would have altered his tone,
And cried, 'These two splinters shall make but one bone.'

W. L. MANSEL

Cheltenham Waters

Here lie I and my four daughters,
Killed by drinking Cheltenham waters.
Had we but stuck to Epsom salts,
We wouldn't have been in these here vaults.

ANON.

The White Knight tells his Tale

I'll tell thee everything I can;
    There's little to relate,
I saw an aged aged man,
    A-sitting on a gate.
'Who are you, aged man?' I said.
    'And how is it you live?'
And his answer trickled through my head
    Like water through a sieve.

He said 'I look for butterflies
    That sleep among the wheat:
I make them into mutton-pies,
    And sell them in the street.
I sell them unto men,' he said,
    'Who sail on stormy seas;
And that's the way I get my bread –
    A trifle, if you please.'

But I was thinking of a plan
    To dye one's whiskers green,
And always use so large a fan
    That they could not be seen.
So, having no reply to give
    To what the old man said,
I cried, ' Come, tell me how you live!'
    And thumped him on the head.

His accents mild took up the tale:
    He said 'I go my ways,
And when I find a mountain-rill,
    I set it in a blaze;
And thence they make a stuff they call
    Rowland's Macassar-Oil –

Yet twopence-halfpenny is all
    They give me for my toil.'

But I was thinking of a way
    To feed oneself on batter,
And so go on from day to day
    Getting a little fatter.
I shook him well from side to side,
    Until his face was blue:
'Come, tell me how you live,' I cried,
    ' And what it is you do!'

He said 'I hunt for haddocks' eyes
    Among the heather bright,
And work them into waistcoat-buttons
    In the silent night.
And these I do not sell for gold
    Or coin of silvery shine,
But for a copper halfpenny,
    And that will purchase nine.

'I sometimes dig for buttered rolls,
    Or set limed twigs for crabs;
I sometimes search the grassy knolls
    For wheels of Hansom-cabs.
And that's the way' (he gave a wink)
    ' By which I get my wealth –
And very gladly will I drink
    Your Honour's noble health.'

I heard him then, for I had just
    Completed my design
To keep the Menai bridge from rust
    By boiling it in wine.
I thanked him much for telling me
    The way he got his wealth,

But chiefly for his wish that he
 Might drink my noble health.

And now, if e'er by chance I put
 My fingers into glue,
Or madly squeeze a right-hand foot
 Into a left-hand shoe,
Or if I drop upon my toe
 A very heavy weight,
I weep, for it reminds me so
Of that old man I used to know —

Whose look was mild, whose speech was slow,
Whose hair was whiter than the snow,
Whose face was very like a crow,
With eyes, like cinders, all aglow,
Who seemed distracted with his woe,
Who rocked his body to and fro,
And muttered mumbingly and low,
As if his mouth were full of dough,
Who snorted like a buffalo —
That summer evening long ago
 A-sitting on a gate.

LEWIS CARROLL

The Old Waiter from Wapping

There was an old waiter from Wapping,
Drew corks for a week without stopping;
 Cried he, 'It's too bad!
 The practice I've had!
Yet cannot prevent them from popping.'

WALTER PARKE

The Owl and the Pussy-Cat

The Owl and the Pussy-Cat went to sea
  In a beautiful pea-green boat,
They took some honey, and plenty of money,
  Wrapped up in a five-pound note.
The Owl looked up to the stars above,
  And sang to a small guitar,
'O lovely Pussy ! O Pussy, my love,
    What a beautiful Pussy you are,
      You are,
      You are!
    What a beautiful Pussy you are!'

Pussy said to the Owl, 'You elegant fowl!
  How charmingly sweet you sing!
O let us be married! too long we have tarried
  But what shall we do for a ring?'
They sailed away for a year and a day,
  To the land where the Bong-tree grows,
And there in a wood a Piggy-wig stood,
    With a ring at the end of his nose,
      His nose,
      His nose,
    With a ring at the end of his nose.

'Dear Pig, are you willing to sell for one shilling
  Your ring?' Said the Piggy, 'I will.'
So they took it away, and were married next day
  By the Turkey who lives on the hill.
They dined on mince, and slices of quince,
  Which they ate with a runcible spoon;
And hand in hand, on the edge of the sand,

They danced by the light of the moon,
  The moon,
  The moon,
They danced by the light of the moon.

EDWARD LEAR

The Pobble who has no Toes

The Pobble who has no toes
  Had once as many as we;
When they said, 'Some day you may lose them all;' –
He replied, – 'Fish fiddle de-dee!'
And his Aunt Jobiska made him drink,
Lavender water tinged with pink,
For she said, 'The World in general knows
There's nothing so good for a Pobble's toes!'
The Pobble who has no toes,
  Swam across the Bristol Channel;
But before he set out he wrapped his nose
  In a piece of scarlet flannel.
For his Aunt Jobiska said, 'No harm
Can come to his toes if his nose is warm;
And it's perfectly known that a Pobble's toes
Are safe, – provided he minds his nose.'
The Pobble swam fast and well,
  And when boats or ships came near him
He tinkledy-binkledy-winkled a bell,
  So that all the world could hear him.
And all the Sailors and Admirals cried,
When they saw him nearing the further side, –
'He has gone to fish, for his Aunt Jobiska's
Runcible Cat with crimson whiskers!'
But before he touched the shore,
  The shore of the Bristol Channel,

A sea-green Porpoise carried away
   His wrapper of scarlet flannel.
And when he came to observe his feet,
Formerly garnished with toes so neat,
His face at once became forlorn
On perceiving that all his toes were gone!
And nobody ever knew
   From that dark day to the present,
Whoso had taken the Pobble's toes,
   In a manner so far from pleasant.
Whether the shrimps or crawfish gray,
Or crafty Mermaids stole them away —
Nobody knew; and nobody knows
How the Pobble was robbed of his twice five toes!
The Pobble who has no toes
   Was placed in a friendly Bark,
And they rowed him back, and carried him up,
   To his Aunt Jobiska's Park.
And she made him a feast at his earnest wish
Of eggs and buttercups fried with fish; —
And she said, — 'It's a fact the whole world knows,
That Pobbles are happier without their toes.'

EDWARD LEAR

The Young Lady in White

There was a Young Lady in White,
Who looked out at the depths of the Night;
   But the birds of the air,
   Filled her heart with despair,
And oppressed that Young Lady in White.

EDWARD LEAR

The Megalopsychiad

Great and good is the typical Don, and of evil and wrong the foe,
Good, and great, I'm a Don myself, and therefore I ought to know:
But of all the sages I ever have met, and of all the Dons I've known,
There never was one so good and great as Megalopsychus Brown.

Megalopsychus Brown was blessed with a Large and Liberal View:
Six sides he saw of a question vexed, when commonplace men saw
    two:
He looked at it East, and he looked at it West, and he looked at it
    upside down –
Such was the large and liberal mind of Megalopsychus Brown.
He held one creed which he made for himself, and he held it fast and
    strong –
That to act in an obvious logical cause is shallow, and base, and
    wrong;
And all that was said for Freedom of Trade so plausible seemed and
    plain,
That he nearly made up his mind to vote for Mr Chamberlain –
Yes! if any one urged that the moon was a cheese, he would always
    at once admit,
Though the point of view was undoubtedly new, there was much
    to be said for it.
But out and alas! for his charity wide had a tendency sad to see
(And it much impaired the practical use of Megalopsychus B.); –
For since, as I've said, no strange ideas could cause him the least
    alarm,
As he never believed that anyone else intended the smallest harm,
He became the sport and the natural prey of men both bold and bad
Who hadn't at heart the Highest Good (as Megalopsychus had);
Men with a crank, and men with a fad, and men with an axe to
    grind,
Men with an eye to the main main chance and an unacademical
    mind.

They told him of Science, they told him of Greek, they told him of
     verses and prose,
They led him about in the strangest ways by his highly respectable
     nose: —

Till the Public awoke and was pained to find that Megalopsychus'
     rule
Had changed what once was the Muses' seat to a kind of Technical
     School;
And everyone said when that learned spot was shorn of its old
     renown,
'Behold the large and liberal views of Megalopsychus Brown!'

A. D. GODLEY

On a Tired Housewife

Here lies a poor woman who was always tired,
She lived in a house where help wasn't hired:
Her last words on earth were: 'Dear friends, I am going
To where there's no cooking, or washing, or sewing,
For everything there is exact to my wishes,
For where they don't eat there's no washing of dishes.
I'll be where loud anthems will always be ringing,
But having no voice I'll be quit of the singing.
Don't mourn for me now, don't mourn for me never,
I am going to do nothing for ever and ever.'

ANON.

Henry King

WHO CHEWED BITS OF STRING, AND WAS EARLY CUT OFF IN DREADFUL AGONIES

The Chief Defect of Henry King
Was chewing little bits of String.
At last he swallowed some which tied
Itself in ugly Knots inside.
Physicians of the Utmost Fame
Were called at once; but when they came
They answered, as they took their Fees,
'There is no Cure for this Disease.
Henry will very soon be dead.'
His Parents stood about his Bed
Lamenting his Untimely Death,
When Henry, with his Latest Breath,
Cried 'Oh, my Friends, be warned by me,
That Breakfast, Dinner, Lunch, and Tea
Are all the Human Frame requires . . .'
With that, the Wretched Child expires.

HILAIRE BELLOC

Matilda

WHO TOLD LIES, AND WAS BURNED TO DEATH

Matilda told such Dreadful Lies,
It made one Gasp and Stretch one's Eyes;
Her Aunt, who, from her Earliest Youth,
Had kept a Strict Regard for Truth,
Attempted to Believe Matilda:
The effort very nearly killed her,
And would have done so, had not She

Discovered this Infirmity.
For once, towards the Close of Day,
Matilda, growing tired of play,
And finding she was left alone,
Went tiptoe to the Telephone
And summoned the Immediate **Aid**
Of London's Noble Fire-Brigade.
Within an hour the Gallant Band
Were pouring in on every hand,
From Putney, Hackney Downs, and Bow.
With Courage high and Hearts a-glow,
They galloped, roaring through the Town,
'Matilda's House is Burning Down!'
Inspired by British Cheers and Loud
Proceeding from the Frenzied Crowd,
They ran their ladders through a score
Of windows on the Ball-Room Floor;
And took Peculiar Pains to Souse
The Pictures up and down the House,
Until Matilda's Aunt succeeded
In showing them they were not needed;
And even then she had to pay
To get the Men to go away!

It happened that a few Weeks later
Her Aunt was off to the Theatre
To see that Interesting Play
The Second Mrs Tanqueray.
She had refused to take her Niece
To hear this Entertaining Piece:
A Deprivation Just and Wise
To Punish her for Telling Lies.
That Night a Fire *did* break out –
You should have heard Matilda Shout!
You should have heard her Scream and Bawl,
And throw the window up and call

To People passing in the Street —
(The rapidly increasing Heat
Encouraging her to obtain
Their confidence) — but all in vain!
For every time She shouted 'Fire!'
They only answered 'Little Liar!'
And therefore when her Aunt returned,
Matilda, and the House, were Burned.

HILAIRE BELLOC

Lord Lundy

WHO WAS TOO FREELY MOVED TO TEARS, AND THEREBY
RUINED HIS POLITICAL CAREER

Lord Lundy from his earliest years
Was far too freely moved to Tears.
For instance, if his Mother said,
'Lundy! It's time to go to Bed!'
He bellowed like a Little Turk.
Or if his father, Lord Dunquerque
Said, 'Hi!' in a Commanding Tone,
'Hi, Lundy! Leave the Cat alone!'
Lord Lundy, letting go its tail,
Would raise so terrible a wail,
As moved His Grandpapa the Duke
To utter the severe rebuke:
'When I, Sir! was a little Boy,
An Animal was not a Toy!'
His father's Elder Sister, who
Was married to a Parvenoo,
Confided to Her Husband, 'Drat
The Miserable, Peevish Brat!
Why don't they drown the Little Beast?'
Suggestions which, to say the least,

Are not what we expect to hear
From Daughters of an English Peer.
His grandmamma, His Mother's Mother,
Who had some dignity or other,
The Garter, or no matter what,
I can't remember all the Lot!
Said, 'Oh! that I were Brisk and Spry
To give him that for which to cry!'
(An empty wish, alas! for she
Was Blind and nearly ninety-three).
The Dear Old Butler thought — but there!
I really neither know nor care
For what the Dear Old Butler thought!
In my opinion, Butlers ought
To know their place, and not to play
The Old Retainer night and day.
I'm getting tired and so are you,
Let's cut the Poem into two!

HILAIRE BELLOC

Lord Lundy

SECOND CANTO

It happened to Lord Lundy then,
As happens to so many men:
Towards the age of twenty-six,
They shoved him into politics;
In which profession he commanded
The income that his rank demanded
In turn as Secretary for
India, the Colonies, and War.
But very soon his friends began
To doubt if he were quite the man:
Thus, if a member rose to say

(As members do, from day to day),
'Arising out of that reply . . .!'
Lord Lundy would begin to cry.
A hint at harmless little jobs
Would shake him with convulsive sobs.
While as for Revelations, these
Would simply bring him to his knees,
And leave him whimpering like a child.
It drove his Colleagues raving wild!
They let him sink from Post to Post,
From fifteen hundred at the most
To eight, and barely six – and then
To be Curator of Big Ben! . . .
And finally there came a Threat
To oust him from the Cabinet!

The Duke – his aged grandsire – bore
The shame till he could bear no more.
He rallied his declining powers,
Summoned the youth to Brackley Towers,
And bitterly addressed him thus –
'Sir! you have disappointed us!
We had intended you to be
The next Prime Minister but three:
The stocks were sold; the Press was squared;
The Middle Class was quite prepared.
But as it is! . . . My language fails!
Go out and govern New South Wales!'

The Aged Patriot groaned and died:
And gracious! how Lord Lundy cried!

HILAIRE BELLOC

The Microbe

The Microbe is so very small
You cannot make him out at all,
But many sanguine people hope
To see him through a microscope.
His jointed tongue that lies beneath
A hundred curious rows of teeth;
His seven tufted tails with lots
Of lovely pink and purple spots,
On each of which a pattern stands,
Composed of forty separate bands;
His eyebrows of a tender green;
All these have never yet been seen –
But Scientists, who ought to know,
Assure us that they must be so . . .
Oh! let us never, never doubt
What nobody is sure about!

HILAIRE BELLOC

On Lady Poltagrue, a Public Peril

The Devil, having nothing else to do,
Went off to tempt My Lady Poltagrue.
My Lady, tempted by a private whim,
To his extreme annoyance, tempted him.

HILAIRE BELLOC

On His Books

When I am dead, I hope it may be said:
'His sins were scarlet, but his books were read.'

HILAIRE BELLOC

Polka

'Tra la la la –
        See me dance the polka,'
Said Mr Wagg like a bear,
'With my top hat
And my whiskers that –
(Tra la la la) trap the Fair.

Where the waves seem chiming haycocks
I dance the polka; there
Stand Venus' children in their gay frocks –
Maroon and marine – and stare

To see me fire my pistol
Through the distance blue as my coat;
Like Wellington, Byron, the Marquis of Bristol,
Buzbied great trees float.

While the wheezing hurdy-gurdy
Of the marine wind blows me
To the tune of Annie Rooney, sturdy,
Over the sheafs of the sea;

And bright as a seedsman's packet
With zinnias, candytufts chill,
Is Mrs Marigold's jacket
As she gapes at the inn door still,

Where at dawn in the box of the sailor,
Blue as the decks of the sea,
Nelson awoke, crowed like the cocks,
Then back to dust sank he.

And Robinson Crusoe
Rues so
The bright and foxy beer –
But he finds fresh isles in a Negress' smiles
The poxy doxy dear,

As they watch me dance the polka,'
Said Mr Wagg like a bear,
'In my top hat and my whiskers that –
Tra la la la, trap the Fair.

Tra la la la la –
Tra la la la la –
Tra la la la la la la la la
                La
                La
                La!'

EDITH SITWELL

I Do Like to Be Beside the Seaside

When
            Don
Pasquito arrived at the seaside
Where the donkey's hide tide brayed, he
Saw the banditto Jo in a black cape
Whose black shape waved like the sea –
Thetis wrote a treatise noting wheat is silver like the sea; the lovely
        cheat is sweat as foam; Erotis notices that she
                Will
                Steal
                The
Wheat-King's luggage, like Babel
Before the League of Nations grew –
So Jo put the luggage and the label

In the pocket of Flo the Kangaroo.
Through trees like rich hotels that bode
Of dreamless ease fled she,
Carrying the load and goading the road
Through the marine scene to the sea.
'Don Pasquito, the road is eloping
With your luggage, though heavy and large;
You must follow and leave your moping
Bride to my guidance and charge!'

When
         Don
Pasquito returned from the road's end,
Where vanilla-coloured ladies ride
From Sevilla, his mantilla'd bride and young friend
Were forgetting their mentor and guide.
For the lady and her friend from Le Touquet
In the very shady trees upon the sand
Were plucking a white satin bouquet
Of foam, while the sand's brassy band
Blared in the wind. Don Pasquito
Hid where the leaves drip with sweet ...
But a word stung him like a mosquito ...
For what they hear, they repeat!

EDITH SITWELL

Forgive me, Sire

Forgive me, sire, for cheating your intent,
That I, who should command a regiment,
Do amble amicably here, O God,
One of the neat ones in your awkward squad.

NORMAN CAMERON

Elegy for Mr Goodbeare

Do you remember Mr Goodbeare, the carpenter,
Godfearing and bearded Mr Goodbeare,
Who worked all day
At his carpenter's tray,
Do you remember Mr Goodbeare?
Mr Goodbeare, that Golconda of gleaming fable,
Lived, thin-ground between orchard and stable,
Pressed thus close against Alfred, his rival –
Mr Goodbeare, who had never been away.

Do you remember Mr Goodbeare,
Mr Goodbeare, who never touched a cup?
Do you remember Mr Goodbeare,
Who remembered a lot?

    Mr Goodbeare could remember
        When things were properly kept up:
    Mr Goodbeare could remember
        The christening and the coming-of-age:
    Mr Goodbeare could remember
        The entire and roasted ox:
    Mr Goodbeare could remember
        When the horses filled the stable,
And the port-wine coloured gentry rode after the tawny fox:
    Mr Goodbeare could remember
        The old lady in her eagle rage,
            Which knew no bounds.
    Mr Goodbeare could remember
        When the escaped and hungering tiger
Flickered lithe and fierce through Foxton Wood,
When old Sir Nigel took his red-tongued, clamouring hounds,
And hunted it then and there,
        As a Gentleman should.

Do you remember Mr Goodbeare,
Mr Goodbeare who never forgot?
Do you remember Mr Goodbeare,
That wrinkled and golden apricot,
Dear, bearded, godfearing Mr Goodbeare
Who remembered remembering such a lot?

Oh, do you remember, do you remember,
As *I* remember and deplore,
That day in drear and far-away December
When dear, godfearing, bearded Mr Goodbeare
Could remember
No more!

                                        SIR OSBERT SITWELL

What Mrs Southern Liked

Mrs Southern was too mild a name
For Dust's Arch-enemy,
Too mild a name
For such a bitterly-sweet activity.
There should have been more of the touch of the east wind in it.

For half a century this grey typhoon
Harried and hurried the girls if they tarried,
And worried and flurried them till they scurried along.
She was always,
                    She said,
Catching them at it,
Loitering as if there was nothing to do,
And laughing, too. She'd teach them
To laugh, she would.
It wasn't for the Likes of Them to laugh.

A lot of loitering, lardy-dardy lazybones
She called them.
Thus she reprimanded and rebuked and scolded,
And scored their names, placing against them
Imaginative but opprobrious epithets,
Specially applicable to girls, moulded
With an accusing index finger
In any dust she found
On table or on window pane.

Slave to the Lares and Penates
Of other people,
She had no wish to stray outside;
Too busy in perpetual conflict
Ever to visit Mr Southern in his market-garden,
She felt no lure of light or trees or flowers.
No:
     What she liked was
               Workmanship.
A cairngorm juggled into the rough likeness of Queen Victoria's
      head, on one side,
And an elephant upon the other:
A negro's face in ebony
      Just like a negro:
A woven tree
      Just like a tree:
A picture of a butcher's shop
      Just like a butcher's shop:
With a mangy dog slinking away with a bone
      Just like a dog that slinks away with a bone:
The marble dimples in a marble baby's knuckle
      Just like the dimples in a baby's knuckle –
        'That,'
      She would confide to Mrs Hague,
'Is where the Hi-talians'
    (That strange, exclamatory and emotional race)

'Have got us beat.
You would know it for a baby's knuckle *anywhere*.'
   (Alarming thought for children
      To find a marble baby's marble knuckle
Thus wandering in the void.)

SIR OSBERT SITWELL

A Caliban

Barely he moved – and read but as he ran;
  To make from sow's ears omelettes he would try,
Cast the last straw upon a drowning man,
  Or pluck the beam from out a needle's eye.

GEOFFREY TAYLOR

Epigram of Straw

It is easier for a drowning man
  To make bricks on the back of a camel than
For a rich man to know
  Which way the winds blow.
Who'd flirt with Threadneedle Street yet flatter Mt Zion
Has bitten off more of the bed than he can lie on.

GEOFFREY TAYLOR

What's the Use?

Sure, deck your lower limbs in pants;
Yours are the limbs, my sweeting.
You look divine as you advance –
Have you seen yourself retreating?

OGDEN NASH

Macavity: The Mystery Cat

Macavity's a Mystery Cat: he's called the Hidden Paw —
For he's the master criminal who can defy the Law.
He's the bafflement of Scotland Yard, the Flying Squad's despair:
For when they reach the scene of crime — Macavity's not there!

Macavity, Macavity, there's no one like Macavity,
He's broken every human law, he breaks the law of gravity.
His powers of levitation would make a fakir stare,
And when you reach the scene of crime — Macavity's not there!
You may seek him in the basement, you may look up in the air —
But I tell you once and once again, Macavity's not there!

Macavity's a ginger cat, he's very tall and thin;
You would know him if you saw him, for his eyes are sunken in.
His brow is deeply lined with thought, his head is highly domed;
His coat is dusty from neglect, his whiskers are uncombed.
He sways his head from side to side, with movements like a snake;
And when you think he's half asleep, he's always wide awake.

Macavity, Macavity, there's no one like Macavity,
For he's a fiend in feline shape, a monster of depravity.
You may meet him in a by-street, you may see him in the square —
But when a crime's discovered, then Macavity's not there!

He's outwardly respectable. (They say he cheats at cards.)
And his footprints are not found in any file of Scotland Yard's.
And when the larder's looted, or the jewel-case is rifled,
Or when the milk is missing, or another Peke's been stifled,
Or the greenhouse glass is broken, and the trellis past repair —
Ay, there's the wonder of the thing! Macavity's not there!

And when the Foreign Office finds a Treaty's gone astray,
Or the Admiralty lose some plans and drawings by the way,

There may be a scrap of paper in the hall or on the stair –
But it's useless to investigate – Macavity's not there!
And when the loss has been disclosed, the Secret Service say:
'It must have been Macavity!' – but he's a mile away.
You'll be sure to find him resting, or a-licking of his thumbs,
Or engaged in doing complicated long division sums.

Macavity, Macavity, there's no one like Macavity,
There never was a Cat of such deceitfulness and suavity.
He always has an alibi, and one or two to spare:
At whatever time the deed took place – MACAVITY WASN'T
    THERE!
And they say that all the Cats whose wicked deeds are widely
    known
(I might mention Mungojerrie, I might mention Griddlebone)
Are nothing more than agents for the Cat who all the time
Just controls their operations: the Napoleon of Crime!

T. S. ELIOT

Buttons

    There was an old skinflint of Hitching
      Had a cook, Mrs Casey, of Cork;
      There was nothing but crusts in the kitchen,
        While in parlour was sherry and pork.
So at last Mrs Casey, her pangs to assuage,
    Having snipped off his buttonses, curried the page;
    And now, while that skinflint gulps sherry and pork
      In his parlour adjacent to Hitching,
To the tune blithe and merry of knife and of fork,
    Anthropophagy reigns in the kitchen.

WALTER DE LA MARE

archy the cockroach says

now and then
there is a person born
who is so unlucky
that he runs into accidents
which started out to happen
to somebody else.

i suppose the human race
is doing the best it can
but hells bells thats
only an explanation
it's not an excuse.

germs are very
objectionable to men
but a germ
thinks of a man
as only the swamp
in which
he has to live.

a louse i
used to know
told me that
millionaires and
bums tasted
about alike
to him.

(*A Maxim*)
if you will drink
hair restorer follow

every dram with some
good standard
depilatory
as a chaser.

DON MARQUIS

The Lesser Lynx

The laughter of the lesser Lynx
   Is often insincere:
It pays to be polite, he thinks,
   If Royalty is near.

So when the Lion steals his food
   Or kicks him from behind,
He smiles, of course – but oh, the rude
   Remarks that cross his mind!

E. V. RIEU

Slug

Slugs, soft upon damp carpets of rich food,
Make sullen love with bubbles and with sighs,
Silvery flaccid. They consider lewd
The use of eyes.

JOHN PUDNEY

Horny Hogan

A FEELTHY POME

Critchers! Horny Hogan sayed
& walked his beat – beat his walk
& saw loif larf, loif cree –
Critchers! Horny scorfed, and spart.

Oi arm the cocker here! Moi
brarss poilished & moi gon in order
Oi arm the cocker, mocker, bocker,
jocker of em all.

Bibies, little winch, twinty-foive
pinnies fer a chonk of luv –
lovers, sodgers, shoppers, sharpers,
mogs pinny-woise & por

lil ones so hoi what nid pertixion –
Oi arm the cocker here! Horny
Hogan sayed. Oi'll sive the larsies,
Oi'll kip the fithe!

Didee? Did Horny Hogan kip it?
Did Horny Hogan kip the larsies
sife and sound from ivil? Woulduv,
rilly woulduv but that he loiked to flarndle

Loiked to flup too much, did Horny,
fer a cop, perticted blonduns,
riduns & brunettes, gave em
the long orm of the lar

Overdid it somut, did Cocker
Mocker Horny Hogan – gave full pertixion to
one too miny ridid, one too miny
blornde – did it ifter hours ivin

till the Force foundim daid one
cool sprin mornin, still pertictin, still
kipin the fithe, shot at his post in a

tinth strit room, the horsband disappeared
& the blornde there wippin –
Horny Hogan daid! Horny
Hogan – kipper of the fithe

Horny Hogan, the cocker mocker of em all.

x   x   x

ROBERT LOWRY

The Turtle

The turtle lives 'twixt plated decks
Which practically conceal its sex.
I think it clever of the turtle
In such a fix to be so fertile.

OGDEN NASH

Samson Agonistes

I test my bath before I sit,
And I'm always moved to wonderment
That what chills the finger not a bit
Is so frigid upon the fundament.

OGDEN NASH

UNLIKELY STORIES

A Carman's Account of a Law-Suit

Marry, I lent my gossip my mare, to fetch home coals
And he her drowned into the quarry holes;
And I ran to the Consistory, for to 'plain,
And there I happened among a greedy meine.
They gave me first a thing they call Citandum;
Within eight days, I got but Libellandum;
Within a month, I got Ad opponendum;
In half a year, I got Interloquendum;
And then I got – how call ye it? – Ad replicandum.
But I could never one word yet understand them;
And then, they caused me cast out many placks,
And made me pay for four-and-twenty acts.
But, ere they came half gait to Concludendum,
The fiend one plack was left for to defend him.
Thus they postponed me two years, with their train,
Then, hodie ad octo, bade me come again,
And then, these rooks, they roupit wonder fast,
For sentence silver, they cried at the last.
Of Pronunciandum they made me wonder fain;
But I got never my good grey mare again.

SIR DAVID LINDESAY

Epitaph on a Welsh Man

Here lyes buryed under these stones,
Shon ap Williams, ap Shinkin, ap Shones,
Her was born in Whales, her was kill'd in France,
Her went to Cot by a very mis-shance.

La yee now.

ANON.

All's Well That Ends Well

A Friend of mine was married to a scold,
To me he came, and all his troubles told.
Said he, 'She's like a woman raving mad.'
'Alas! my friend,' said I, 'that's very bad!'
'No, not so bad,' said he; 'for, with her, true
I had both house and land, and money too.'
    'That was well,' said I;
    'No, not so well,' said he;
    'For I and her own brother
    Went to law with one another;
    I was cast, the suit was lost,
And every penny went to pay the cost.'
    'That was bad,' said I;
    'No, not so bad,' said he:
'For we agreed that he the house should keep,
And give to me four score of Yorkshire sheep
All fat, and fair, and fine, they were to be.'
'Well, then,' said I, 'sure that was well for thee?'
    'No, not so well,' said he;
    'For, when the sheep I got,
    They every one died of the rot.'
    'That was bad,' said I;
    'No, not so bad,' said he;
    'For I had thought to scrape the fat
    And keep it in an oaken vat;
Then into tallow melt for winter store.'
'Well, then,' said I, 'that's better than before?'
    ' 'Twas not so well,' said he;
    'For having got a clumsy fellow
    To scrape the fat and melt the tallow;
Into the melting fat the fire catches,
    And, like brimstone matches,
    Burnt my house to ashes.'

'That was bad,' said I;
'No! not so bad,' said he; 'for, what is best,
My scolding wife has gone among the rest.'

ANON.

Nullum, Stimulum Ignoris

Caecus, awake, was told the Sun appear'd
Which had the darkness of the morning clear'd:
But Caecus, sluggish, thereto makes reply,
'The sun hath further far to go than I.'

ANON.

Scylla Toothlesse

Scylla is toothlesse; yet when she was young,
She had both tooth enough, and too much tongue:
What should I now of toothlesse Scylla say?
But that her tongue hath worne her teeth away.

ANON.

The Doctor Prescribes

A lady lately, that was fully sped
Of all the pleasures of the marriage-bed
Ask'd a physician, whether were more fit
For Venus' sports, the morning or the night?
The good old man made answer, as 'twas meet,
The morn more wholesome, but the night more sweet.
Nay then, i' faith, quoth she, since we have leisure,
We'll to't each morn for health, each night for pleasure.

ANON.

Paulo Purganti and his Wife

AN HONEST, BUT A SIMPLE PAIR

A Doctor of great Skill and Fame,
PAULO PURGANTI was his Name,
Had a good, comely, virtuous Wife:
No Woman led a better Life:
She to Intrigues was ev'n hard-hearted:
She chuckl'd when a Bawd was carted:
And thought the Nation ne'er wou'd thrive,
Till all the Whores were burnt alive.

On marry'd Men, that dare be bad,
She thought no Mercy should be had;
They should be hang'd, or starv'd, or flead,
Or serv'd like Romish Priests in Swede. –
In short, all Lewdness She defy'd:
And stiff was her Parochial Pride.

Yet in an honest Way, the Dame
Was a great Lover of That same;
And could from Scripture take her Cue,
That Husbands should give Wives their Due.

Her Prudence did so justly steer
Between the Gay and the Severe,
That if in some Regards She chose
To curb poor PAULO in too close;
In others She relax'd again,
And govern'd with a looser Rein.

Thus tho' She strictly did confine
The Doctor from Excess of Wine;

With Oysters, Eggs, and Vermicelli
She let Him almost burst his Belly:
Thus drying Coffee was deny'd;
But Chocolate that Loss supply'd:
And for Tobacco (who could bear it?)
Filthy Concomitant of Claret!
(Blest Revolution!) one might see
Eringo Roots, and Bohé Tea.

She often set the Doctor's Band,
And strok'd his Beard, and squeez'd his Hand:
Kindly complain'd, that after Noon
He went to pore on Books too soon:
She held it wholesomer by much,
To rest a little on the Couch: —
About his Waste in Bed a-nights
She clung so close — for fear of Sprites.

The Doctor understood the Call;
But had not always wherewithal.

The Lion's Skin too short, you know,
(As Plutarch's Morals finely show)
Was lengthen'd by the Fox's Tail:
And Art supplies, where Strength may fail.

Unwilling then in Arms to meet
The Enemy, He could not beat;
He strove to lengthen the Campaign,
And save his Forces by Chicane.
Fabius, the Roman Chief, who thus
By fair Retreat grew Maximus,
Shows us, that all that Warrior can do
With Force inferior, is *Cunctando*.

One Day then, as the Foe drew near,
With Love, and Joy, and Life, and Dear;
Our Don, who knew this Tittle Tattle
Did, sure as Trumpet, call to Battel;
Thought it extremely *à propos*,
To ward against the coming Blow:
To ward: but how? Ay, there's the Question:
Fierce the Assault, unarm'd the Bastion.

The Doctor feign'd a strange Surprise:
He felt her Pulse: he view'd her Eyes:
That beat too fast: These rowl'd too quick:
She was, He said, or would be Sick:
He judg'd it absolutely good,
That She should purge and clense her Blood.
SPAW Waters for that end were got:
If they past easily or not,
What matters it? the Lady's Feaver
Continu'd violent as ever.

For a Distemper of this Kind,
(BLACKMORE and HANS are of my Mind)
If once it youthful Blood infects,
And chiefly of the Female Sex;
Is scarce remov'd by Pill or Potion;
What-e'er might be our Doctor's Notion.

One luckless Night then, as in Bed
The Doctor and the Dame were laid;
Again this cruel Feaver came,
High Pulse, short Breath, and Blood in Flame.
What Measures shall poor PAULO keep
With Madam, in this piteous taking?
She, like MACBETH, has murder'd Sleep,

And won't allow Him Rest, tho' waking.
Sad State of Matters! when We dare
Nor ask for Peace, nor offer War:
Nor LIVY nor COMINES have shown,
What in this Juncture may be done.
GROTIUS might own, that PAULO's Case is
Harder, than any which He places
Amongst his BELLI and his PACIS.

He strove, alas! but strove in vain,
By dint of Logic to maintain,
That all the Sex was born to grieve,
Down to her Ladyship from EVE.
He rang'd his Tropes, and preach'd up Patience;
Back'd his Opinion with Quotations,
Divines and Moralists; and run ye on
Quite thro' from SENECA to BUNYAN.
As much in vain He bid Her try
To fold her Arms, to close her Eye;
Telling Her, Rest would do Her Good;
If any thing in Nature cou'd:
So held the GREEKS quite down from GALEN,
Masters and Princes of the Calling:
So all our Modern Friends maintain
(Tho' no great GREEKS) in WARWICK-LANE.

Reduce, my Muse, the wand'ring Song:
A Tale should never be too long.

The more He talk'd, the more She burn'd,
And sigh'd, and tost, and groan'd, and turn'd:
At last, I wish, said She, my Dear —
(And whisper'd something in his Ear.)
You wish! wish on, the Doctor cries:

Lord! when will Womankind be wise?
What, in your Waters? are You mad?
Why Poyson is not half so bad.
I'll do it – But I give you Warning:
You'll die before To-morrow Morning. –
'Tis kind, my Dear, what You advise;
The Lady with a Sigh replies:
But Life, You know, at best is Pain:
And Death is what We should disdain.
So do it therefore, and Adieu:
For I will die for Love of You: –
Let wanton Wives by Death be scar'd:
But, to my Comfort, I'm prepar'd.

MATTHEW PRIOR

Hans Carvel

HANS CARVEL, Impotent and Old,
Married a Lass of LONDON Mould:
Handsome? enough; extreamly Gay:
Lov'd Musick, Company, and Play:
High Flights She had, and Wit at Will:
And so her Tongue lay seldom still:
For in all Visits who but She,
To Argue, or to Repartée?

She made it plain, that Human Passion
Was order'd by Predestination;
That, if weak Women went astray,
Their Stars were more in Fault than They:
Whole Tragedies She had by Heart:
Enter'd into ROXANA'S Part:

To Triumph in her Rival's Blood,
The Action certainly was good.
How like a Vine young AMMON curl'd!
Oh that dear Conqu'ror of the World!
She pity'd BETTERTON in age,
That ridicul'd the God-like Rage.

She, first of all the Town, was told,
Where newest INDIA Things were sold
So in a Morning, without Bodice,
Slipt sometimes out to Mrs THODY'S;
To cheapen Tea, to buy a Screen:
What else cou'd so much Virtue mean?
For to prevent the least Reproach,
Betty went with Her in the Coach.

But when no very great Affair
Excited her peculiar Care;
She without fail was wak'd at Ten;
Drank Chocolate, then slept again:
At Twelve She rose: with much ado
Her Cloaths were huddl'd on by Two:
Then; Does my Lady Dine at home?
Yes sure; – but is the Colonel come?
Next, how to spend the Afternoon,
And not come Home again too soon;
The Change, the City, or the Play,
As each was proper for the Day;
A Turn in Summer to HYDE-PARK,
When it grew tolerably Dark.

Wife's Pleasure causes Husband's Pain:
Strange Fancies come in HANS'S Brain:
He thought of what He did not name;

And wou'd reform; but durst not blame.
At first He therefore Preach'd his Wife
The Comforts of a Pious Life:
Told Her, how Transient Beauty was;
That All must die, and Flesh was Grass:
He bought Her Sermons, Psalms, and Graces;
And doubled down the useful Places.
But still the Weight of worldly Care
Allow'd Her little time for Pray'r:
And CLEOPATRA was read o'er,
While SCOT, and WAKE, and Twenty more,
That teach one to deny one's self,
Stood unmolested on the Shelf.
An untouch'd Bible grac'd her Toilet:
No fear that Thumb of Her's should spoil it.
In short, the Trade was still the same:
The Dame went out: the Colonel came.

What's to be done? poor CARVEL cry'd:
Another Batt'ry must be try'd:
What if to Spells I had Recourse?
'Tis but to hinder something Worse.
The End must justifie the Means:
He only Sins who Ill intends:
Since therefore 'tis to Combat Evil;
'Tis lawful to employ the Devil.

Forthwith the Devil did appear
(For name Him and He's always near)
Not in the Shape in which He plies
At Miss's Elbow when She lies;
Or stands before the Nurs'ry Doors,
To take the naughty Boy that roars:
But without Sawcer Eye or Claw,
Like a grave Barrister at Law.

HANS CARVEL, lay aside your Grief,
The Devil says: I bring Relief.
Relief, says HANS: pray let me crave
Your Name, Sir. – SATAN. – Sir, your Slave:
I did not look upon your Feet:
You'll pardon Me: – Ay, now I see't:
And pray, Sir, when came You from Hell?
Our Friends there, did You leave Them well?
All well: but pr'ythee, honest HANS,
(Says SATAN) leave your Complaisance:
The Truth is this: I cannot stay
Flaring in Sun-shine all the Day:
For, *entre Nous*, We Hellish Sprites,
Love more the Fresco of the Nights;
And oft'ner our Receipts convey
In Dreams, than any other Way.
I tell You therefore as a Friend,
Ere Morning dawns, your Fears shall end:
Go then this Ev'ning, Master CARVEL,
Lay down your Fowls, and broach your Barrel;
Let Friends and Wine dissolve your Care;
Whilst I the great Receipt prepare:
To Night I'll bring it, by my Faith;
Believe for once what SATAN saith.

Away went HANS: glad? not a little;
Obey'd the Devil to a Tittle;
Invited Friends some half a Dozen,
The Colonel, and my Lady's Cousin.
The Meat was serv'd; the Bowls were crown'd;
Catches were sung; and Healths went round:
Barbadoes Waters for the Close;
'Till Hans had fairly got his Dose:
The Colonel toasted to the best:
The Dame mov'd off, to be undrest:
The Chimes went Twelve: the Guests withdrew:

But when, or how, HANS hardly knew.
Some Modern Anecdotes aver,
He nodded in his Elbow Chair;
From thence was carry'd off to Bed:
JOHN held his Heels, and NAN his head.
My Lady was disturb'd: new Sorrow!
Which HANS must answer for to Morrow.

In Bed then view this happy Pair;
And think how HYMEN Triumph'd there.
Hans, fast asleep, as soon as laid;
The Duty of the Night unpaid:
The waking Dame, with Thoughts opprest,
That made Her Hate both Him and Rest:
By Such a Husband, such a Wife!
'Twas ACME'S and SEPTIMIUS' Life.
The Lady sigh'd: the Lover snor'd:
The punctual Devil kept his Word:
Appear'd to honest HANS again;
But not at all by Madam seen:
And giving Him a Magick Ring,
Fit for the Finger of a King;
Dear Hans, said He, this Jewel take,
And wear it long for SATAN'S Sake:
'Twill do your Business to a Hair:
For long as You this Ring shall wear,
As sure as I look over LINCOLN,
That ne'er shall happen which You think on.

HANS took the Ring with Joy extream;
(All this was only in a Dream)
And thrusting it beyond his Joint,
'Tis done, He cry'd: I've gain'd my Point. —
What Point, said She, You ugly Beast?
You neither give Me Joy nor Rest:

'Tis done. – What's done, You drunken Bear?
You've thrust your Finger G – d knows where.

MATTHEW PRIOR

On Hall's Death

AN EPIGRAM

Poor HALL caught his death standing under a spout,
Expecting till midnight when NAN would come out,
But fatal his patience, as cruel the Dame,
And curst was the Weather that quench'd the man's flame.

'Who e'er thou art, that read'st these moral lines,
Make love at home, and go to bed betimes.'

MATTHEW PRIOR

Bibo

AN EPIGRAM

When BIBO thought fit from the world to retreat,
As full of Champagne as an egg's full of meat,
He wak'd in the boat; and to CHARON he said,
He wou'd be row'd back, for he was not yet dead.
Trim the boat, and sit quiet, stern CHARON reply'd:
You may have forgot, you were drunk when you dy'd.

MATTHEW PRIOR

The Knife-Grinder

FRIEND OF HUMANITY:

'Needy Knife-grinder! whither are you going?
Rough is the road – your wheel is out of order –
Bleak blows the blast; your hat has got a hole in't,
                          So have your breeches!

'Weary Knife-grinder! little think the proud ones,
Who in their coaches roll along the turnpike -
Road, what hard work 'tis crying all day "Knives and
                          Scissors to grind O!"

'Tell me, Knife-grinder, how you came to grind knives?
Did some rich man tyrannically use you?
Was it the squire? or parson of the parish?
                          Or the attorney?

'Was it the squire, for killing of his game? or
Covetous parson, for his tithes distraining?
Or roguish lawyer, made you lose your little
                          All in a law-suit?

'(Have you not read the Rights of Man, by Tom Paine?)
Drops of compassion tremble on my eyelids,
Ready to fall, as soon as you have told your
                          Pitiful story.'

KNIFE-GRINDER:

'Story! God bless you! I have none to tell, sir,
Only last night, a-drinking at the Chequers,
This poor old hat and breeches, as you see, were
                          Torn in a scuffle.

'Constables came up for to take me into
Custody; they took me before the justice;

Justice Oldmixon put me in the parish-
      Stocks for a vagrant.

'I should be glad to drink your Honour's health in
A pot of beer, if you will give me sixpence;
But for my part, I never love to meddle
      With politics, sir.'

FRIEND OF HUMANITY:
 'I give thee sixpence! I will see thee damn'd first –
 Wretch! whom no sense of wrongs can rouse to vengeance –
 Sordid, unfeeling, reprobate, degraded,
      Spiritless outcast!'

(*Kicks the Knife-grinder, overturns his wheel, and exit in a transport
of Republican enthusiasm and universal philanthropy.*)

         GEORGE CANNING

Of All the Men

 Of all the men one meets about,
  There's none like Jack – he's everywhere:
 At church – park – auction – dinner – rout –
  Go when and where you will, he's there.
 Try the West End, he's at your back –
  Meets you, like Eurus, in the East –
 You're call'd upon for 'How do, Jack?'
  One hundred times a day, at least.
 A friend of his one evening said,
  As home he took his pensive way,
 'Upon my soul, I fear Jack's dead –
  I've seen him but three times to-day!'

         THOMAS MOORE
           c 2

An Actor

A shabby fellow chanced one day to meet
The British Roscius in the street,
   Garrick, of whom our nation justly brags;
The fellow hugged him with a kind embrace ; –
'Good sir, I do not recollect your face,'
   Quoth Garrick. 'No?' replied the man of rags;
'The boards of Drury you and I have trod
   Full many a time together, I am sure.'
'When?' with an oath, cried Garrick, 'for, by G – d,
I never saw that face of yours before!
   What characters, I pray,
   Did you and I together play?'
'Lord!' quoth the fellow, 'think not that I mock –
When you played Hamlet, sir, I played the cock!'

PETER PINDAR (JOHN WOLCOT)

On Uncle Peter Dan'els

Beneath this stone, a lump of clay,
   Lies Uncle Peter Dan'els,
Who, early in the month of May,
   Took off his winter flannels.

ANON.

On a Hampshire Grenadier

Here sleeps in peace a Hampshire grenadier,
Who caught his death by drinking cold small beer.
Soldiers be wise from his untimely fall,
And when you're hot drink strong or not at all.

ANON.

Misadventures at Margate

A LEGEND OF JARVIS'S JETTY

(Mr Simpkinson loquitur)

I was in Margate last July, I walk'd upon the pier,
I saw a little vulgar Boy – I said, 'What make you here? –
The gloom upon your youthful cheek speaks any thing but joy';
Again I said, 'What make you here, you little vulgar Boy?'

He frown'd, that little vulgar Boy – he deem'd I meant to scoff:
And when the little heart is big, a little 'sets it off';
He put his finger in his mouth, his little bosom rose, –
He had no little handkerchief to wipe his little nose!

'Hark! don't you hear, my little man? – it's striking nine,' I said,
'An hour when all good little boys and girls should be in bed.
Run home and get your supper, else your Ma' will scold – Oh!
        fie! –
It's very wrong indeed for little boys to stand and cry!'

The tear-drop in his little eye again began to spring,
His bosom throbb'd with agony – he cried like any thing!
I stoop'd, and thus amidst his sobs I heard him murmur – 'Ah
I haven't got no supper! and I haven't got no Ma'!! –

'My father, he is on the seas, – my mother's dead and gone!
And I am here, on this here pier, to roam the world alone;
I have not had, this live-long day, one drop to cheer my heart,
Nor "brown" to buy a bit of bread with, – let alone a tart.

'If there's a soul will give me food, or find me in employ,
By day or night, then blow me tight!' (he was a vulgar Boy);
'And now I'm here, from this here pier it is my fixed intent
To jump, as Mister Levi did from off the Monu-ment!'

'Cheer up! cheer up! my little man – cheer up!' I kindly said.
'You are a naughty boy to take such things into your head:
If you should jump from off the pier, you'd surely break your legs,
Perhaps your neck – then Bogey'd have you, sure as eggs are eggs!

'Come home with me, my little man, come home with me and sup;
My landlady is Mrs Jones – we must not keep her up –
There's roast potatoes on the fire, – enough for me and you –
Come home, you little vulgar Boy – I lodge at Number 2.'

I took him home to Number 2, the house beside 'The Foy'
I bade him wipe his dirty shoes – that little vulgar Boy, –
And then I said to Mistress Jones, the kindest of her sex,
'Pray be so good as go and fetch a pint of double X!'

But Mrs Jones was rather cross, she made a little noise,
She said she 'did not like to wait on little vulgar Boys.'
She with her apron wiped the plates, and, as she rubb'd the delf,
Said I might 'go to Jericho, and fetch my beer myself!'

I did not go to Jericho – I went to Mr Cobb –
I changed a shilling – (which in town the people call 'a Bob') –
It was not so much for myself as for that vulgar child –
And I said, 'A pint of double X, and please to draw it mild!'

When I came back I gazed about – I gazed on stool and chair –
I could not see my little friend – because he was not there!
I peep'd beneath the table-cloth – beneath the sofa too –
I said 'You little vulgar Boy! why what's become of you?'

I could not see my table-spoons – I look'd, but could not see
The little fiddle-pattern'd ones I use when I'm at tea;
– I could not see my sugar-tongs – my silver watch – oh, dear!
I know 'twas on the mantel-piece when I went out for beer.

I could not see my Mackintosh! – it was not to be seen!
Nor yet my best white beaver hat, broad-brimm'd and lined with
	green;
My carpet-bag – my cruet-stand, that holds my sauce and soy, –
My roast potatoes! – all are gone! – and so's that vulgar Boy!

I rang the bell for Mrs Jones, for she was down below,
' – Oh, Mrs Jones! what do you think? – ain't this a pretty go?
– That horrid little vulgar Boy whom I brought here to-night,
– He's stolen my things and run away! !' – Says she, 'And sarve
	you right! !'

*

Next morning I was up betimes – I sent the Crier round,
All with his bell and gold-laced hat, to say I'd give a pound
To find that little vulgar Boy, who'd gone and used me so;
But when the Crier cried 'O Yes!' the people cried, 'O No!'

I went to 'Jarvis' Landing-place,' the glory of the town,
There was a common sailor-man a-walking up and down;
I told my tale – he seem'd to think I'd not been treated well,
And called me 'Poor old Buffer!' – what that means I cannot tell.

That sailor-man, he said he'd seen that morning on the shore,
A son of – something – 'twas a name I'd never heard before,
A little 'gallows-looking chap' – dear me; what could he mean?
With a 'carpet-swab' and 'muckingtogs,' and a hat turned up with
	green.

He spoke about his 'precious eyes,' and said he'd seen him 'sheer,'
– It's very odd that sailor-men should talk so very queer –
And then he hitch'd his trousers up, as is, I'm told, their use,
– It's very odd that sailor-men should wear those things so loose.

I did not understand him well, but think he meant to say
He'd seen that little vulgar Boy, that morning swim away
In Captain Large's Royal George about an hour before,
And they were now, as he supposed, 'some*wheres*' about the Nore.

A landsman said, 'I *twig* the chap – he's been upon the Mill –
And 'cause he *gammons* so the flats, ve calls him Veeping Bill!'
He said 'he'd done me wery brown,' and 'nicely *stow'd* the *swag*.'
– That's French, I fancy, for a hat – or else a carpet-bag.

I went and told the constable my property to track;
He asked me if 'I did not wish that I might get it back!'
I answered, 'To be sure I do! – it's what I come about.'
He smiled and said, 'Sir, does your mother know that you are out?'

Not knowing what to do, I thought I'd hasten back to town,
And beg our own Lord Mayor to catch the Boy who'd 'done me
      brown.'
His Lordship very kindly said he'd try and find him out,
But he 'rather thought that there were several vulgar boys about.'

He sent for Mr Withair then, and I described 'the swag,'
My Mackintosh, my sugar-tongs, my spoons, and carpet-bag;
He promised that the New Police should all their powers employ;
But never to this hour have I beheld that vulgar Boy!

Moral

Remember, then, what when a boy I've heard my Grandma' tell,
'BE WARN'D IN TIME BY OTHERS' HARM, AND YOU SHALL DO
    FULL WELL!'
Don't link yourself with vulgar folks, who've got no fix'd abode,
Tell lies, use naughty words, and say they 'wish they may be
    blow'd!'

Don't take too much of double X! – and don't at night go out
To fetch your beer yourself, but make the pot-boy bring your
      stout!
And when you go to Margate next, just stop and ring the bell,
Give my respects to Mrs Jones, and say I'm pretty well!

R. H. BARHAM

The Sorrows of Werther

Werther had a love for Charlotte
    Such as words could never utter;
Would you know how first he met her?
    She was cutting bread and butter.

Charlotte was a married lady,
    And a moral man was Werther,
And for all the wealth of Indies,
    Would do nothing for to hurt her.

So he sigh'd and pined and ogled,
    And his passion boil'd and bubbled,
Till he blew his silly brains out,
    And no more was by it troubled.

Charlotte, having seen his body
    Borne before her on a shutter,
Like a well-conducted person,
    Went on cutting bread and butter.

W. M. THACKERAY

Plain Language from Truthful James

I reside at Table Mountain, and my name is Truthful James;
I am not up to small deceit, or any sinful games;
And I'll tell in simple language what I know about the row
That broke up our Society upon the Stanislow.

But first I would remark, that it is not a proper plan
For any scientific gent to whale his fellow-man,
And, if a member don't agree with his peculiar whim,
To lay for that same member for to 'put a head' on him.

Now nothing could be finer or more beautiful to see
Than the first six months' proceedings of that same Society,
Till Brown of Calaveras brought a lot of fossil bones
That he found within a tunnel near the tenement of Jones.

Then Brown he read a paper, and he reconstructed there,
From those same bones, an animal that was extremely rare;
And Jones then asked the Chair for a suspension of the rules,
Till he could prove that those same bones was one of his lost mules.

Then Brown he smiled a bitter smile, and said he was at fault,
It seemed he had been trespassing on Jones's family vault;
He was a most sarcastic man, this quiet Mr Brown,
And on several occasions he had cleaned out the town.

Now I hold it is not decent for a scientific gent
To say another is an ass – at least, to all intent;
Nor should the individual who happens to be meant
Reply by heaving rocks at him to any great extent.

Then Abner Dean of Angel's raised a point of order, when
A chunk of old red sandstone took him in the abdomen,
And he smiled a kind of sickly smile, and curled up on the floor,
And the subsequent proceedings interested him no more.

For, in less time than I write it, every member did engage
In a warfare with the remnants of a palaeozoic age;
And the way they heaved those fossils in their anger was a sin,
Till the skull of an old mammoth caved the head of Thompson in.

And this is all I have to say of these improper games,
For I live at Table Mountain, and my name is Truthful James;
And I've told in simple language what I knew about the row
That broke up our Society upon the Stanislow.

BRET HARTE

The Heathen Chinee

Which I wish to remark –
    And my language is plain –
That for ways that are dark
    And for tricks that are vain,
The heathen Chinee is peculiar,
    Which the same I would rise to explain.

Ah Sin was his name;
    And I shall not deny
In regard to the same
    What that name might imply;
But his smile it was pensive and child-like,
    As I frequent remarked to Bill Nye.

It was August the third;
    And quite soft was the skies.
Which it might be inferred
    That Ah Sin was likewise;
Yet he played it that day upon William
    And me in a way I despise.

Which we had a small game,
    And Ah Sin took a hand:
It was Euchre. The same
    He did not understand;
But he smiled as he sat by the table,
    With the smile that was child-like and bland.

Yet the cards they were stocked
    In a way that I grieve,
And my feelings were shocked
    At the state of Nye's sleeve:
Which was stuffed full of aces and bowers,
    And the same with intent to deceive.

But the hands that were played
    By that heathen Chinee,
And the points that he made,
    Were quite frightful to see, –
Till at last he put down a right bower,
    Which the same Nye had dealt unto me.

Then I looked up at Nye,
    And he gazed upon me;
And he rose with a sigh,
    And said, 'Can this be?
We are ruined by Chinese cheap labour,'
    And he went for that heathen Chinee.

In the scene that ensued
    I did not take a hand,
But the floor it was strewed
    Like the leaves on the strand
With the cards that Ah Sin had been hiding,
    In the game 'he did not understand'.

In his sleeves, which were long,
    He had twenty-four packs, –
Which was coming it strong,
    Yet I state but the facts;
And we found on his nails, which were taper,
    What is frequent in tapers, – that's wax.

Which is why I remark,
    And my language is plain,
That for ways that are dark,
    And for tricks that are vain,
The heathen Chinee is peculiar –
    Which the same I am free to maintain.

BRET HARTE

On Johnny Cole

Here lies Johnny Cole,
Who died, on my soul,
After eating a plentiful dinner;
While chewing his crust,
He was turned into dust,
With his crimes undigested – poor sinner.

ANON.

On Mary Ann

Mary Ann has gone to rest,
Safe at last on Abraham's breast,
Which may be nuts for Mary Ann,
But is certainly rough on Abraham.

ANON.

The Two Old Bachelors

Two old Bachelors were living in one house;
One caught a Muffin, the other caught a Mouse.
Said he who caught the Muffin to him who caught the Mouse, –
'This happens just in time, for we've nothing in the house,
Save a tiny slice of lemon and a teaspoonful of honey,
And what to do for dinner, – since we haven't any money?
And what can we expect if we haven't any dinner,
But to lose our teeth and eyelashes and keep on growing thinner?'

Said he who caught the Mouse to him who caught the Muffin, –
'We might cook this little Mouse if we only had some Stuffin'!
If we had but Sage and Onions we could do extremely well,
But how to get that Stuffin' it is difficult to tell!'

Those two old Bachelors ran quickly to the town
And asked for Sage and Onions as they wandered up and down;
They borrowed two large Onions, but no Sage was to be found
In the Shops or in the Market or in all the Gardens round.

But some one said, – 'A hill there is, a little to the north,
And to its purpledicular top a narrow way leads forth; –
And there among the rugged rocks abides an ancient Sage, –
An earnest Man, who reads all day a most perplexing page.
Climb up and seize him by the toes! – all studious as he sits, –
And pull him down, and chop him into endless little bits!
Then mix him with your Onion (cut up likewise into scraps),
And your Stuffin' will be ready, and very good – perhaps.'

Those two old Bachelors, without loss of time,
The nearly purpledicular crags at once began to climb;
And at the top among the rocks, all seated in a nook,
They saw that Sage a-reading of a most enormous book.

'You earnest Sage!' aloud they cried, 'your book you've read
      enough in! –
We wish to chop you into bits and mix you into Stuffin'!' –
But that old Sage looked calmly up, and with his awful book
At those two Bachelors' bald heads a certain aim he took; –
And over crag and precipice they rolled promiscuous down, –
At once they rolled, and never stopped in lane or field or town;
And when they reached their house, they found (besides their want
      of Stuffin')
The Mouse had fled; – and previously had eaten up the Muffin.

They left their home in silence by the once convivial door;
And from that hour those Bachelors were never heard of more.

EDWARD LEAR

The Young Lady of Lucca

There was a Young Lady of Lucca,
Whose lovers completely forsook her;
    She ran up a tree,
    And said, 'Fiddle-de-dee!'
Which embarrassed the people of Lucca.

EDWARD LEAR

The Young Lady of Tyre

There was a Young Lady of Tyre,
Who swept the loud chords of a lyre;
    At the sound of each sweep
    She enraptured the deep,
And enchanted the city of Tyre.

EDWARD LEAR

Muddled Metaphors

Oh, ever thus from childhood's hour
 I've seen my fondest hopes recede!
I never loved a tree or flower
 That didn't trump its partner's lead.

I never nursed a dear gazelle,
 To glad me with its dappled hide,
But when it came to know me well
 It fell upon the buttered side.

I never taught a cockatoo
 To whistle comic songs profound,
But just when 'Jolly Dogs' it knew
 It failed for ninepence in the pound.

I never reared a walrus cub
 In my aquarium to plunge,
But, when it learnt to love its tub,
 It placidly threw up the sponge.

I never strove a metaphor
 To every bosom home to bring,
But — just as it had reached the door —
 It went and cut a pigeon's wing.

THOMAS HOOD, JR.

A Syllogizing Philosopher

You, reasoning, play but ball with a pretence;
 Tattered in logic, every question beg.
I answer you according to my sense,
 Friday is faster, far, than a fried egg.
  With words bone-dry you'll try to knot thought's mesh;
  But are bones dry, quick-lodging in live flesh?

GEOFFREY TAYLOR

Shake, Mulleary and Go-ethe

I have a bookcase, which is what
Many much better men have not.
There are no books inside, for books,
I am afraid, might spoil its looks,
But I've three busts, all second-hand,
Upon the top. You understand
I could not put them underneath —
Shake, Mulleary and Go-ethe.

Shake was a dramatist of note;
He lived by writing things to quote,
He long ago put on his shroud:
Some of his works are rather loud.
His bald-spot's dusty, I suppose.
I know there's dust upon his nose.
I'll have to give each nose a sheath —
Shake, Mulleary and Go-ethe.

Mulleary's line was quite the same;
He has more hair, but far less fame.
I would not from that fame retrench —
But he is foreign, being French.
Yet high his haughty head he heaves,
The only one done up in leaves,
They're rather limited on wreath —
Shake, Mulleary and Go-ethe.

Go-ethe wrote in the German tongue:
He must have learned it very young.
His nose is quite a butt for scoff,
Although an inch of it is off.
He did quite nicely for the Dutch;
But here he doesn't count for much.
They all are off their native heath —
Shake, Mulleary and Go-ethe.

They sit there, on their chests, as bland
As if they were not second-hand.
I do not know of what they think,
Nor why they never frown or wink.
But why from smiling they refrain
I think I clearly can explain:
They none of them could show much teeth –
Shake, Mulleary and Go-ethe.

H. C. BUNNER

Epitaph on a Geologist

Where shall we our great professor inter
    That in peace he may rest his bones?
If we hew him a rocky sepulchre,
    He'll rise and break the stones,
And examine each stratum that lies around,
For he's quite in his element under ground.

If with mattock and spade his body we lay
    In the common alluvial soil,
He'll start up and snatch those tools away,
    Of his own geological toil;
In a stratum so young the professor disdains
That embedded should be his organic remains.

Thus expos'd to the drop of some case-hard'ning spring
    His carcase let stalactite cover :
And to Oxford the petrified sage let us bring,
    When he is encrusted all over:
Then 'mid mammoths and crocodiles, high on a shelf,
Let him stand as a monument rais'd to himself.

ANON.

· *Hans Breitmann's Barty*

Hans Breitmann gife a barty;
 Dey had biano-blayin',
I felled in lofe mit a Merican frau,
 Her name vas Madilda Yane.
She hat haar as prown ash a pretzel,
 Her eyes vas himmel-plue,
Und vhen dey looket indo mine,
 Dey shplit mine heart in dwo.

Hans Breitmann gife a barty,
 I vent dere you'll pe pound;
I valtzet mit Madilda Yane,
 Und vent shpinnen' round und round.
De pootiest Fraulein in de house,
 She vayed 'pout dwo hoondred pound,
Und efery dime she gife a shoomp
 She make de vindows sound.

Hans Breitmann gife a barty,
 I dells you it cost him dear;
Dey rolled in more ash sefen keeks
 Of foost-rate lager beer.
Und vhenefer dey knocks de shpicket in
 De Deutschers gifes a cheer;
I dinks dot so vine a barty
 Nefer coom to a het dis year.

Hans Breitmann gife a barty;
 Dere all vas Souse and Brouse,
Vhen de sooper comed in, de gompany
 Did make demselfs to house;
Dey ate das Brot and Gensy broost,
 De Bratwurst and Braten vine,

Und vash der Abendessen down
    Mit four parrels of Neckarwein.

Hans Breitmann gife a barty;
    Ve all cot troonk ash bigs.
I poot mine mout' to a parrel of beer,
    Und emptied it oop mit a schwigs;
Und den I gissed Madilda Yane,
    Und she shlog me on de kop,
Und de gompany vighted mit daple-lecks
    Dill de coonshtable made oos shtop.

Hans Breitmann gife a barty –
    Vhere ish dot barty now?
Vhere ish de lofely golden cloud
    Dot float on de moundain's prow?
Vhere ish de himmelstrahlende Stern –
    De shtar of de shpirit's light?
All goned afay mit de lager beer –
    Afay in de Ewigkeit!

C. G. LELAND

On a Wag in Mauchline

Lament him, Mauchline husbands a',
    He often did assist ye;
For had ye staid whole weeks awa',
    Your wives they ne'er had missed ye.

Ye Mauchline bairns, as on ye pass,
    To school in bands thegither,
Oh, tread ye lightly on his grass,
    Perhaps he was your father.

ROBERT BURNS

The Owl-Critic

'Who stuffed that white owl?' No one spoke in the shop.
The barber was busy, and he couldn't stop;
The customers, waiting their turns, were all reading
The 'Daily,' the 'Herald,' the 'Post', little heeding
The young man who blurted out such a blunt question;
No one raised a head, or even made a suggestion;
　　　　　And the barber kept on shaving.

'Don't you see, Mr Brown,'
Cried the youth, with a frown,
'How wrong the whole thing is,
How preposterous each wing is,
How flattened the head is, how jammed down the neck is —
In short, the whole owl, what an ignorant wreck 't is!
I make no apology;
I've learned owl-eology.

'I've passed days and nights in a hundred collections,
And cannot be blinded to any deflections
Arising from unskilful fingers that fail
To stuff a bird right, from his beak to his tail.
Mister Brown! Mister Brown!
Do take that bird down,
Or you'll soon be the laughing-stock all over town!'
　　　　　And the barber kept on shaving.

'I've studied owls,
And other night-fowls,
And I tell you
What I know to be true;
An owl cannot roost
With his limbs so unloosed:

No owl in this world
Ever had his claws curled,
Ever had his legs slanted,
Ever had his bill canted,
Ever had his neck screwed
Into that attitude.
He can't do it, because
'Tis against all bird-laws.

'Anatomy teaches,
Ornithology preaches,
An owl has a toe
That can't turn out so!
I've made the white owl my study for years,
And to see such a job almost moves me to tears!
Mr Brown, I'm amazed
You should be so gone crazed
As to put up a bird
In that posture absurd!
To look at that owl really brings on a dizziness;
The man who stuffed him don't half know his business!'
          And the barber kept on shaving.

'Examine those eyes.
I'm filled with surprise
Taxidermists should pass
Off on you such poor glass;
So unnatural they seem
They'd make Audubon scream,
And John Burroughs laugh
To encounter such chaff.
Do take that bird down;
Have him stuffed again, Brown!'
          And the barber kept on shaving.

'With some sawdust and bark
I could stuff in the dark
An owl better than that.
I could make an old hat
Look more like an owl
Than that horrid fowl,
Stuck up there so stiff like a side of coarse leather.
In fact, about him there's not one natural feather.'

Just then, with a wink and a sly normal lurch,
The owl, very gravely, got down from his perch,
Walked round, and regarded his fault-finding critic
(Who thought he was stuffed) with a glance analytic,
And then fairly hooted, as if he should say:
'Your learning's at fault this time, anyway;
Don't waste it again on a live bird, I pray.
I'm an owl; you're another. Sir Critic, good day!'
          And the barber kept on shaving.

J. T. FIELDS

The Japanese

How courteous is the Japanese;
He always says, 'Excuse it, please.'
He climbs into his neighbour's garden,
And smiles, and says, 'I beg your pardon';
He bows and grins a friendly grin,
And calls his hungry family in;
He grins, and bows a friendly bow;
'So sorry, this my garden now.'

OGDEN NASH

The Yarn of the 'Nancy Bell'

'Twas on the shores that round our coast
    From Deal to Ramsgate span,
That I found alone on a piece of stone
    An elderly naval man.

His hair was weedy, his beard was long,
    And weedy and long was he,
And I heard this wight on the shore recite,
    In a singular minor key:

'Oh, I am a cook and a captain bold,
    And the mate of the *Nancy* brig,
And a bo'sun tight, and a midshipmite,
    And the crew of the captain's gig.'

And he shook his fists and he tore his hair,
    Till I really felt afraid,
For I couldn't help thinking the man had been drinking,
    And so I simply said:

'Oh, elderly man, it's little I know
    Of the duties of men of the sea,
And I'll eat my hand if I understand
    How you can possibly be

'At once a cook, and a captain bold,
    And the mate of the *Nancy* brig,
And a bo'sun tight, and a midshipmite,
    And the crew of the captain's gig.'

Then he gave a hitch to his trousers, which
    Is a trick all seamen larn,

And having got rid of a thumping quid,
   He spun this painful yarn:

' 'Twas in the good ship *Nancy Bell*
   That we sailed to the Indian Sea,
And there on a reef we come to grief,
   Which has often occurred to me.

'And pretty nigh all the crew was drowned
   (There was seventy-seven o' soul),
And only ten of the *Nancy's* men
   Said "here" to the muster-roll.

'There was me and the cook and the captain bold,
   And the mate of the *Nancy* brig,
And the bo'sun tight, and a midshipmite,
   And the crew of the captain's gig.

'For a month we'd neither wittles nor drink,
   Till a-hungry we did feel,
So we drawed a lot, and accordin' shot
   The captain for our meal.

'The next lot fell to the *Nancy's* mate,
   And a delicate dish he made;
Then our appetite with the midshipmite
   We seven survivors stayed.

'And then we murdered the bos'un tight,
   And he much resembled pig;
Then we wittled free, did the cook and me,
   On the crew of the captain's gig.

'Then only the cook and me was left,
   And the delicate question, "Which

Of us two goes to the kettle?" arose,
    And we argued it out as sich.

'For I loved that cook as a brother, I did,
    And the cook he worshipped me;
But we'd both be blowed if we'd either be stowed
    In the other chap's hold, you see.

' "I'll be eat if you dines off me," says Tom.
    "Yes, that," says I, "you'll be, –
I'm boiled if I die, my friend," quoth I.
    And "Exactly so," quoth he.

'Says he, "Dear James, to murder me
    Were a foolish thing to do,
For don't you see that you can't cook *me*,
    While I can – and will – cook *you*!"

'So he boils the water, and takes the salt
    And the pepper in portions true
(Which he never forgot), and some chopped shallot,
    And some sage and parsley too.

' "Come here," says he, with a proper pride,
    Which his smiling features tell,
" 'Twill soothing be if I let you see
    How extremely nice you'll smell."

'And he stirred it round and round and round,
    And he sniffed at the foaming froth;
When I ups with his heels, and smothers his squeals
    In the scum of the boiling broth.

'And I eat that cook in a week or less,
    And – as I eating be

The last of his chops, why, I almost drops,
    For a vessel in sight I see.

*

'And I never larf, and I never smile,
    And I never lark or play,
But sit and croak, and a single joke
    I have, – which is to say:

'Oh, I am a cook and a captain bold,
    And the mate of the *Nancy* brig,
And a bos'un tight, and a midshipmite,
    And the crew of the captain's gig.'

SIR W. S. GILBERT

Tender Heartedness

Billy, in one of his nice new sashes,
Fell in the fire and was burnt to ashes;
Now, although the room grows chilly,
I haven't the heart to poke poor Billy.

HARRY GRAHAM

Misfortunes never come Singly

Making toast at the fireside,
Nurse fell in the grate and died;
And what makes it ten times worse,
All the toast was burnt with nurse.

HARRY GRAHAM

The Encounter

Twittingpan seized my arm, though I'd have gone
willingly. To be seen with him alone,
the choicest spirit of the present age,
flattered my vanity into quite a rage.
His was the presence always in dispute
by every cocktail hostess of repute;
and I'd long enjoyed seeing his drooping form
breast each successive, new-aesthetic storm.
He had championed Epstein, Gertrude, and *Parade*,
and even now was nothing of a die-hard;
(I had last heard him on some Red-film show-day
expounding *tonal montage* in the foyer);
being two days nimbler than the smartest clique
he gave the cachet to the safest chic.
    We turned from Regent Street to Conduit Street.
He thought my overcoat was far from neat,
offered his tailor's name and then forgot.
His mind was in a turmoil and overshot
immediate objects in transcendent aims.
Juggling voluptuously with Christian names
he listed for me each new partnership
contracted since I'd given Town the slip
for ten days in the wilds near Sevenoaks;
and Lord! I thought, no wonder Douglas [1] croaks
imminent fire and brimstone; though no Prudhomme,
I could never quite regret the fate of Sodom.
    This intellectual athlete next began
praising the freedom of the modern man
from dogma, morals, and the plagues of nature –
a scientific, half-angelic creature,
immune from all – my hero almost winces –

1. James, not Norman. A vice-hound and highbrow baiter employed by the *Sunday Express*.

Tokyo is down,[1] but dancing's on at Prince's.
He summed up briefly all religion means
and then explained the universe by Jeans.
Burly Jack Haldane next supplied his text
(and as the Sacred Writ is always vext
into queer meanings for sectarian ends),
Twittingpan preached the marriage of true friends
when blessed parthenogenesis arrives
and he-uranians can turn honest wives.

'Consider Bond Street,' as we reached it, cried
falsetto Twittingpan, our period's pride,
'Does it not realise in microcosm
the whole ideal Time nurses in its bosom?
Luxury, cleanliness and objects d'art,
the modern Trinity for us all who are
freed from the burden of the sense of sin.
Lord Russell says . . .' I feared he would begin
an exposition of the free man's worship,
that neo-anabaptist, compelled to dip
not now from mystic but hygienic motives.
'But look, in Shanks's [2] shop the Past still lives;
those gross utensils symbolically bind us
to the brute part we soon shall leave behind us,
for Haldane promises in the world-to-come
excretion's inoffensive minimum.' [3]
He gestured freely and drew inquiring stares
from elegant shoppers wrapped like dainty bears,
whilst I blushed like a country cousin come
to the Time-metropolis from an archaic home.
He saw my red cheeks, and with a kindly air
proclaimed sophistication everywhere.
'You must meet Iris, she who lives serene
in the intense confession of the obscene
and drags her tea-time sex-affair all fresh

1. This refers to the 1923 catastrophe. Also to Voltaire.   2. Sanitary
engineers.   3. See Daedalus.

to the dinner-table, like a cat with flesh.
Her new book is, I hear, just too, *too* topical,
though Janet's peeved not to be in it at all.
But Basil's poems are far more utter than
you can imagine, as you don't know the man.'
With that he handed me a deckled sheet
where these lines staggered on uncertain feet:

> you the one onely
> not more but one than
> two is superfluous two is
> i reminds you of me
> me reminds i of you
> i is another
> identity unidentifiable
> then say is love not
> the word
> all love is perhaps no love
> or is perhaps luck
> or no luck is no love rather.

'Chaste, isn't it? And yes, I must explain
that I inspired it, at risk of seeming vain;
otherwise you might miss its fine notations
which do convey so subtly my relations
with the dear fellow. You two must really meet;
he would impress you even in the street.'
I fixed my look at 'silent admiration'
and paced along all tense with expectation,
though bashful at my Siamese-like linking
with the lank oracle of modern thinking.
　'Lewis and Middleton Murry are, I'm sure,
the only moderns likely to endure
of the older crowd; for Eliot's later works
are merely sanctimonious quips and quirks;
and Huxley is portentously obsessed

with the problems that make City clerks depressed.
Don't you think Wyndham Lewis too divine?
That brute male strength he shows in every line!
I swear if he'd flogged me in his last book but one,
as some kind person informed me he has done,
I'd have forgiven him for the love of art.
And you, too, ought to take his works to heart
as I have done, for torn by inner strife,
I've made him mentor of my mental life.
You cannot imagine what a change that worked.
I who was all emotion, and always shirked
the cold chaste isolation of male mind,
now thrust in front all I had kept behind.
I'd lived in Time and Motion and Sensation,
then smashed my watch and burnt the Bloomsbury *Nation* ...
But here comes Clarence – Clarence with Basil!' So
like a hot poker then he let my arm go;
and, stifling jealousy, hailed them with 'How nice!'
They flaunted gay shirts and a grand old vice.
Poor Twittingpan had no novelty to produce;
I was not shabby enough to be of use
as a quaint genius, nor smart enough for friend.
Poor wretch! To put his agony at an end
I touched my hat, good-day, sir-ed, like a tout,
and left my Twittingpan to lie it out.

EDGELL RICKWORD

Mother Goose's Garland

Around, around the sun we go:
The moon goes round the earth.
We do not die of death:
We die of vertigo.

ARCHIBALD MACLEISH

Willie's Epitaph

Little Willie from his mirror
    Licked the mercury right off,
Thinking, in his childish error,
    It would cure the whooping cough.
At the funeral his mother
    Smartly said to Mrs Brown:
    ' 'Twas a chilly day for Willie
When the mercury went down.'

ANON.

Martyrs: Modern Style

VIDE 'TOTEM AND TABU'

'The Crucifixion is an Incest Myth,
  Christ's blood procures our well-earned doom's reprieve.
It needs intelligence,' claimed Mr Smythe,
  'to know such things, yet, childlike still, believe.

'We cherish simple faith, though it offend
  the saturnalia of this modern Rome.
Good Friday night my wife and I attend
  a Sacred Concert in the Hippodrome.'

EDGELL RICKWORD

Miss Twye

Miss Twye was soaping her breasts in her bath
When she heard behind her a meaning laugh
And to her amazement she discovered
A wicked man in the bathroom cupboard.

GAVIN EWART

FOR VARIOUS
OCCASIONS

Report of an Adjudged Case

Between Nose and Eyes a strange contest arose,
  The spectacles set them unhappily wrong;
The point in dispute was, as all the world knows,
  To which the said spectacles ought to belong.

So Tongue was the lawyer, and argued the cause
  With a great deal of skill, and a wig full of learning;
While chief baron Ear sat to balance the laws
  So famed for his talent in nicely discerning.

In behalf of the Nose it will quickly appear,
  And your lordship, he said, will undoubtedly find,
That the Nose has had spectacles always in wear,
  Which amounts to possession time out of mind.

Then holding the spectacles up to the court –
  Your lordship observes they are made with a straddle,
As wide as the ridge of the Nose is; in short,
  Designed to sit close to it, just like a saddle.

Again, would your lordship a moment suppose
  ('Tis a case that has happen'd, and may be again)
That the visage or countenance had not a Nose,
  Pray who would, or who could, wear spectacles then?

On the whole it appears, and my argument shows,
  With a reasoning the court will never condemn,
That the spectacles plainly were made for the Nose,
  And the Nose was as plainly intended for them.

Then shifting his side, as a lawyer knows how,
　　He pleaded again in behalf of the Eyes:
But what were his arguments few people know,
　　For the court did not think they were equally wise.

So his lordship decreed, with a grave solemn tone,
　　Decisive and clear, without one *if* or *but* –
That, whenever the Nose put his spectacles on,
　　By daylight or candlelight – Eyes should be shut!

WILLIAM COWPER

To the Immortal Memory of the Halibut

ON WHICH I DINED THIS DAY, MONDAY, APRIL 26, 1784

Where hast thou floated, in what seas pursued
Thy pastime? when wast thou an egg new spawn'd,
Lost in th'immensity of ocean's waste?
Roar as they might, the overbearing winds
That rock'd the deep, thy cradle, thou wast safe –
And in thy minikin and embryo state,
Attach'd to the firm leaf of some salt weed,
Didst outlive tempests, such as wrung and rack'd
The joints of many a stout and gallant bark,
And whelm'd them in the unexplored abyss.
Indebted to no magnet and no chart,
Nor under guidance of the polar fire,
Thou wast a voyager on many coasts,
Grazing at large in meadows submarine,
Where flat Batavia, just emerging, peeps
Above the brine – where Caledonia's rocks
Beat back the surge – and where Hibernia shoots
Her wondrous causeway far into the main.
– Wherever thou hast fed, thou little thought'st,

And I not more, that I should feed on thee.
Peace, therefore, and good health, and much good fish
To him who sent thee! and success, as oft
As it descends into the billowy gulf,
To the same drag that caught thee! – Fare thee well!
Thy lot thy brethren of the slimy fin
Would envy, could they know that thou wast doom'd
To feed a bard, and to be praised in verse.

WILLIAM COWPER

Quin's Soliloquy

ON SEEING DUKE HUMPHRY AT ST ALBANS

A Plague on Egypt's arts, I say!
Embalm the dead! on senseless clay
    Rich wines and spices waste!
Like sturgeon, or like brawn, shall I,
Bound in a precious pickle, lie,
    Which I can never taste?

Let me embalm this flesh of mine
With turtle-fat, and Bourdeaux wine,
    And spoil th'Egyptian trade!
Than Humphry's duke more happy I ...
Embalmed alive, old Quin shall die
    A mummy ready made.

DAVID GARRICK

Holy Willie's Prayer

O Thou, wha in the heavens dost dwell,
Wha, as it pleases best Thysel',
Sends ane to Heaven, an' ten to Hell,
   A' for Thy glory,
And no for onie guid or ill
    They've done afore Thee!

I bless and praise Thy matchless might,
Whan thousands Thou hast left in night,
That I am here, afore Thy sight,
   For gifts an' grace,
A burnin' an' a shinin' light
   To a' this place.

What was I, or my generation,
That I should get sic exaltation!
I, wha deserv'd most just damnation,
   For broken laws
Sax thousand years 'fore my creation,
   Thro' Adam's cause.

When frae my mither's womb I fell,
Thou might hae plung'd me deep in Hell,
To gnash my gooms, to weep and wail
   In burnin' lakes,
Whare damnèd devils roar and yell,
   Chain'd to their stakes.

Yet I am here, a chosen sample,
To show Thy grace is great and ample;
I'm here a pillar o' Thy temple,
   Strong as a rock,

A guide, a buckler, an example
    To a' Thy flock!

O Lord, thou kens what zeal I bear,
When drinkers drink, and swearers swear,
And singin' there and dancin' here,
    Wi' great and sma':
For I am keepit by thy fear
    Free frae them a'.

But yet, O Lord! confess I must,
At times I'm fash'd wi' fleshly lust;
An' sometimes, too, in wardly trust,
    Vile self gets in;
But Thou remembers we are dust,
    Defil'd wi' sin.

O Lord, yestreen, thou kens, wi' Meg –
Thy pardon I sincerely beg;
O! may't ne'er be a livin' plaque
    To my dishonour,
An I'll ne'er lift a lawless leg
    Again upon her.

Besides I farther maun allow
Wi' Lizzie's lass, three times I trow –
But, Lord, that Friday I was fou,
    When I cam near her,
Or else thou kens thy servant true
    Wad never steer her.

May be Thou lets this fleshly thorn
Beset Thy servant e'en and morn,
Lest he owre proud and high should turn
    That he's sae gifted:

If sae Thy han' maun e'en be borne
      Until Thou lift it.

Lord, bless Thy chosen in this place,
For here Thou has a chosen race:
But God confound their stubborn face,
      An' blast their name,
Wha' bring Thy elders to disgrace
      An' open shame!

Lord, mind Gawn Hamilton's deserts,
He drinks, an' swears, an' plays at cartes,
Yet has sae monie takin' arts,
      Wi' great and sma',
Frae God's ain priest the people's hearts
      He steals awa.

An' when we chasten'd him therefore,
Thou kens how he bred sic a splore,
As set the warld in a roar
      O' laughin' at us; –
Curse Thou his basket and his store,
      Kail an' potatoes!

Lord, hear my earnest cry and pray'r
Against the Presbyt'ry o' Ayr!
Thy strong right hand, Lord, mak it bare
      Upo' their heads!
Lord, visit them, an' dinna spare,
      For their misdeeds!

O Lord my God! that glib-tongu'd Aiken,
My vera heart and saul are quakin'
To think how we stood sweatin', shakin',
      An' pish'd wi' dread,

While he, wi' hingin' lip an' snakin',
      Held up his head.

Lord, in Thy day o' vengeance try him!
Lord, visit them wha did employ him,
And pass not in Thy mercy by them,
      Nor hear their pray'r;
But for Thy people's sake destroy them,
      An' dinna spare!

But, Lord, remember me and mine,
Wi' mercies temp'ral and divine,
That I for grace and gear may shine,
      Excell'd by nane,
An' a' the glory shall be Thine,
      Amen, Amen!

                ROBERT BURNS

Sonnet

The sky is glowing in one ruddy sheet; —
A cry of fire! resounds from door to door;
And westward still the thronging people pour; —
The turncock hastens to F. P. 6 feet,
And quick unlocks the fountains of the street;
While rumbling engines, with increasing roar,
Thunder along to luckless Number Four,
Where Mr Dough makes bread for folks to eat.
And now through blazing flames, and fiery beams,
The Globe, the Sun, the Phoenix and what not,
With gushing pipes throw up abundant streams,
On burning bricks, and twists, on rolls — too hot —
And scorching loaves, — as if there were no shorter
And cheaper way of making toast and water.

                THOMAS HOOD

Ode to St Swithin

'THE RAIN IT RAINETH EVERY DAY'

The Dawn is overcast, the morning low'rs,
On ev'ry window-frame hang beaded damps
Like rows of small illumination lamps
To celebrate the Jubilee of Show'rs!
A constant sprinkle patters from all leaves,
The very Dryads are not dry, but soppers,
    And from the Houses' eaves
    Tumble eaves-droppers.

The hundred clerks that live along the street,
Bondsmen to mercantile and city schemers,
With squashing, sloshing, and galloshing feet,
Go paddling, paddling, through the wet, like steamers,
Each hurrying to earn the daily stipend –
Umbrellas pass of every shade of green,
And now and then a crimson one is seen
    Like an Umbrella *ripen'd*.

    Over the way a waggon
Stands with six smoking horses, shrinking, blinking,
    While in the George and Dragon
The man is keeping himself dry – and drinking!
The Butcher's boy skulks underneath his tray,
    Hats shine – shoes don't – and down droop collars,
And one blue Parasol cries all the way
    To school, in company with four small scholars!

Unhappy is the man to-day who rides,
Making his journey sloppier, not shorter;
Aye, there they go, a dozen of outsides,
Performing on 'a Stage with real water!'

A dripping Pauper crawls along the way,
  The only real willing out-of-doorer,
  And says, or seems to say,
'Well, I am poor enough – but here's a *pourer*!'

The scene in water colours thus I paint,
Is your own Festival, you Sloppy Saint!
Mother of all the Family of Rainers!
  Saint of the Soakers!
  Making all people croakers,
Like frogs in swampy marshes, and complainers!
And why you mizzle forty days together,
Giving the earth your water-soup to sup,
I marvel – Why such wet, mysterious weather?
  I wish you'd *clear it up*!

  Why cast such cruel dampers
On pretty Pic Nics, and against all wishes
Set the cold ducks a-swimming in the hampers,
And volunteer, unask'd, to wash the dishes?
Why drive the Nymphs from the selected spot,
  To cling like lady-birds around a tree –
  Why spoil a Gipsy party at their tea,
By throwing your cold water upon hot?

Cannot a rural maiden, or a man,
Seek Hornsey-Wood by invitation, sipping
  Their green with Pan,
But souse you come, and show their Pan all dripping!
Why upon snow-white table-cloths and sheets,
That do not wait, or want a second washing,
  Come squashing?
Why task yourself to lay the dust in streets,
As if there were no Water-Cart contractors,
No pot-boys spilling beer, no shop-boys ruddy

Spooning out puddles muddy,
Milkmaids, and other slopping benefactors!

A Queen you are, raining in your own right,
Yet oh! how little flatter'd by report!
    Even by those that seek the Court,
Pelted with every term of spleen and spite.
Folks rail and swear at you in every place;
They say you are a creature of no bowel;
They say you're always washing Nature's face,
    And that you then supply her
        With nothing drier
Than some old wringing cloud by way of towel!
The whole town wants you duck'd, just as you duck it,
They wish you on your own mud porridge supper'd,
They hope that you may kick your own big bucket,
Or in your water-butt go souse! heels up'ard!
They are, in short, so weary of your drizzle,
They'd spill the water in your veins to stop it –
Be warn'd! You are too partial to a mizzle –
        Pray *drop it*!

THOMAS HOOD

Ode on a Distant Prospect of Clapham Academy

Ah me! those old familiar bounds!
That classic house, those classic grounds,
    My pensive thought recalls!
What tender urchins now confine,
What little captives now repine,
    Within you irksome walls?

Ay, that's the very house! I know
Its ugly windows, ten a-row!
    Its chimneys in the rear!

And there's the iron rod so high,
That drew the thunder from the sky,
   And turn'd our table-beer!

There I was birch'd! there I was bred!
There like a little Adam fed
   From Learning's woeful tree!
The weary tasks I used to con! –
The hopeless leaves I wept upon! –
   Most fruitless leaves to me! –

The summon'd class! – the awful bow! –
I wonder who is master now
   And wholesome anguish sheds!
How many ushers now employs,
How many maids to see the boys
   Have nothing in their heads!

And Mrs S * * *? – Doth she abet
(Like Pallas in the parlour) yet
   Some favour'd two or three, –
The little Crichtons of the hour,
Her muffin-medals that devour,
   And swill her prize – bohea?

Ay, there's the play-ground! there's the lime
Beneath whose shade in summer's prime
   So wildly I have read! –
Who sits there *now*, and skims the cream
Of young Romance, and weaves a dream
   Of Love and Cottage-bread?

Who struts the Randall of the walk?
Who models tiny heads in chalk?
   Who scoops the light canoe?
What early genius buds apace?

Where's Poynter? Harris? Bowers? Chase?
  Hal Baylis? blithe Carew?

Alack! they're gone – a thousand ways!
And some are serving in 'the Greys',
    And some have perish'd young! –
Jack Harris weds his second wife;
Hal Baylis drives the wane of life;
    And blithe Carew – is hung!

Grave Bowers teaches A B C
To savages at Owhyee;
    Poor Chase is with the worms! –
All, all are gone – the olden breed! –
New crops of mushroom boys succeed,
    'And push us from our *forms*!'

Lo! where they scramble forth, and shout,
And leap, and skip, and mob about,
    At play where we have play'd!
Some hop, some run (some fall), some twine
Their crony arms; some in the shine,
    And some are in the shade!

Lo! there what mix'd conditions run!
The orphan lad; the widow's son;
    And Fortune's favour'd care –
The wealthy-born, for whom she hath
Mac-Adamized the future path –
    The Nabob's pamper'd heir!

Some brightly starr'd – some evil born, –
For honour some, and some for scorn, –
    For fair or foul renown!
Good, bad, indiff'rent – none may lack!

Look, here's a White, and there's a Black!
   And there's a Creole brown!

Some laugh and sing, some mope and weep,
And wish *their* frugal sires would keep
   Their only sons at home; –
Some tease the future tense, and plan
The full-grown doings of the man,
   And pant for years to come!

A foolish wish! There's one at hoop;
And four at *fives*! and five who stoop
   The marble taw to speed!
And one that curvets in and out,
Reining his fellow Cob about, –
   Would I were in his *steed*!

Yet he would gladly halt and drop
That boyish harness off, to swop
   With this world's heavy van –
To toil, to tug. O little fool!
While thou canst be a horse at school
   To wish to be a man!

Perchance thou deem'st it were a thing
To wear a crown, – to be a king!
   And sleep on regal down!
Alas! thou know'st not kingly cares;
Far happier is thy head that wears
   That hat without a crown!

And dost thou think that years acquire
New added joys? Dost think thy sire
   More happy than his son?
That manhood's mirth? – Oh, go thy ways

To Drury Lane when —— *plays*,
  And see how *forced* our fun!

Thy taws are brave! – thy tops are rare! –
Our tops are spun with coils of care,
  Our *dumps* are no delight! –
The Elgin marbles are but tame,
And 'tis at best a sorry game
  To fly the Muse's kite!

Our hearts are dough, our heels are lead,
Our topmost joys fall dull and dead
  Like balls with no rebound!
And often with a faded eye
We look behind, and send a sigh
  Towards that merry ground!

Then be contented. Thou hast got
The most of heaven in thy young lot;
  There's sky-blue in thy cup!
Thou'lt find thy Manhood all too fast –
Soon come, soon gone! and Age at last
  A sorry *breaking-up*!

THOMAS HOOD

The Old Loony of Lyme

There was an old loony of Lyme,
Whose candour was simply sublime;
  When they asked, 'Are you there?'
  'Yes,' he said, 'but take care,
For I'm never "all there" at a time.'

ANON.

Garden Fancies

SIBRANDUS SCHAFNABURGENSIS

Plague take all your pedants, say I!
    He who wrote what I hold in my hand,
Centuries back was so good as to die,
    Leaving this rubbish to cumber the land;
This, that was a book in its time,
    Printed on paper and bound in leather,
Last month in the white of a matin-prime
    Just when the birds sang all together.

Into the garden I brought it to read,
    And under the arbute and laurustine
Read it, so help me grace in my need,
    From title-page to closing line.
Chapter on chapter did I count,
    As a curious traveller counts Stonehenge;
Added up the mortal amount;
    And then proceeded to my revenge.

Yonder's a plum-tree with a crevice
    An owl would build in, were he but sage;
For a lap of moss, like a fine pont-levis
    In a castle of the Middle Age,
Joins to a lip of gum, pure amber;
    When he'd be private, there might he spend
Hours alone in his lady's chamber:
    Into this crevice I dropped our friend.

Splash, went he, as under he ducked,
    At the bottom, I knew, rain-drippings stagnate:
Next, a handful of blossoms I plucked
    To bury him with, my bookshelf's magnate;

Then I went in-doors, brought out a loaf,
  Half a cheese, and a bottle of Chablis;
Lay over the grass and forgot the oaf
  Over a jolly chapter of Rabelais.

Now, this morning, betwixt the moss
  And gum that locked our friend in limbo,
A spider had spun his web across,
  And sat in the midst with arms akimbo.
So I took pity, for learning's sake,
  And, *de profundis, accentibus laetis,*
Cantate! quoth I, as I got a rake;
  And up I fished his delectable treatise.

Here you have it, dry in the sun,
  With all the binding all of a blister,
And great blue spots where the ink has run,
  And reddish streaks that wink and glister
O'er the page so beautifully yellow:
  Oh, well have the droppings played their tricks!
Did he guess how toadstools grow, this fellow?
  Here's one stuck in his chapter six!

How did he like it when the live creatures
  Tickled and toused and browsed him all over,
And worm, slug, eft, with serious features,
  Came in, each one, for his right of trover?
— When the water-beetle with great blind deaf face
  Made of her eggs the stately deposit,
And the newt borrowed just so much of the preface
  As tiled in the top of his black wife's closet?

All that life and fun and romping,
  All that frisking and twisting and coupling,
While slowly our poor friend's leaves were swamping
  And clasps were cracking and covers suppling!

As if you had carried sour John Knox
    To the play-house at Paris, Vienna or Munich,
Fastened him into a front-row box,
    And danced off the ballet with trousers and tunic.

Come, old martyr! What, torment enough is it?
    Back to my room shall you take your sweet self.
Goodbye, mother-beetle; husband-eft, *sufficit!*
    See the snug niche I have made on my shelf!
A's book shall prop you up, B's shall cover you,
    Here's C to be grave with, or D to be gay,
And with E on each side, and F right over you,
    Dry-rot at ease till the Judgement-day!

ROBERT BROWNING

A Practical Answer

Says Hyam to Moses,
'Let's cut off our noses'
Says Moses to Hyam
'Ma tear, who vould buy 'em?'

SHIRLEY BROOKS

On a Magazine Sonnet

'Scorn not the sonnet', though its strength be sapped,
    Nor say malignant its inventor blundered;
The corpse that here in fourteen lines is wrapped
    Had otherwise been covered with a hundred.

R. H. LOINES

Beer

In those old days which poets say were golden –
   (Perhaps they laid the gilding on themselves:
And, if they did, I'm all the more beholden
   To those brown dwellers in my dusty shelves,
Who talk to me 'in language quaint and olden'
   Of gods and demigods and fauns and elves,
Pan with his pipes, and Bacchus with his leopards,
And staid young goddesses who flirt with shepherds:)

In those old days, the Nymph called Etiquette
   (Appalling thought to dwell on) was not born.
They had their May, but no Mayfair as yet,
   No fashions varying as the hues of morn.
Just as they pleased they dressed and drank and ate,
   Sang hymns to Ceres (their John Barleycorn)
And danced unchaperoned, and laughed unchecked,
And were no doubt extremely incorrect.

Yet do I think their theory was pleasant:
   And oft, I own, my 'wayward fancy roams'
Back to those times, so different from the present;
   When no one smoked cigars, nor gave At-homes,
Nor smote a billiard-ball, nor winged a pheasant,
   Nor 'did' her hair by means of long-tailed combs,
Nor migrated to Brighton once a year,
Nor – most astonishing of all – drank Beer.

No, they did not drink Beer, 'which brings me to'
   (As Gilpin said) 'the middle of my song.'
Not that 'the middle' is precisely true,
   Or else I should not tax your patience long:
If I had said 'beginning' it might do;
   But I have a dislike to quoting wrong:

I was unlucky – sinned against, not sinning –
When Cowper wrote down 'middle' for 'beginning'.

So to proceed. That abstinence from Malt
    Has always struck me as extremely curious.
The Greek mind must have had some vital fault,
    That they should stick to liquors so injurious –
(Wine, water, tempered p'raps with Attic salt) –
    And not at once invent that mild, luxurious,
And artful beverage, Beer. How the digestion
Got on without it, is a startling question.

Had they digestions? and an actual body
    Such as dyspepsia might make attacks on?
Were they abstract ideas – (like Tom Noddy
    And Mr Briggs) – or men, like Jones and Jackson?
Then nectar – was that beer, or whisky-toddy?
    Some say the Gaelic mixture, I the Saxon:
I think a strict adherence to the latter
Might make some Scots less pigheaded, and fatter.

Besides, Bon Gaultier definitely shows
    That the real beverage for feasting gods on
Is a soft compound, grateful to the nose
    And also to the palate, known as 'Hodgson'.
I know a man – a tailor's son – who rose
    To be a peer: and this I would lay odds on,
(Though in his memoirs it may not appear,)
That that man owed his rise to copious Beer.

O Beer! O Hodgson, Guinness, Allsopp, Bass!
    Names that should be on every infant's tongue!
Shall days and months and years and centuries pass,
    And still your merits be unrecked, unsung?
Oh! I have gazed into my foaming glass,
    And wished that lyre could yet again be strung

Which once rang prophet-like through Greece, and taught her
Misguided sons that the best drink was water.

How would he now recant that wild opinion,
    And sing – as would that I could sing – of you!
I was not born (alas!) the 'Muses' minion',
    I'm not poetical, not even blue:
And he, we know, but strives with waxen pinion,
    Who'er he is that entertains the view
Of emulating Pindar, and will be
Sponsor at last to some now nameless sea.

Oh! when the green slopes of Arcadia burned
    With all the lustre of the dying day,
And on Cithaeron's brow the reaper turned,
    (Humming, of course, in his delightful way,
How Lycidas was dead, and how concerned
    The Nymphs were when they saw his lifeless clay;
And how rock told to rock the dreadful story
That poor young Lycidas was gone to glory:)

What would that lone and labouring soul have given,
    At that soft moment for a pewter pot!
How had the mists that dimmed his eye been riven,
    And Lycidas and sorrow all forgot!
If his own grandmother had died unshriven,
    In two short seconds he'd have recked it not;
Such power hath Beer. The heart which Grief hath canker'd
Hath one unfailing remedy – the Tankard.

Coffee is good, and so no doubt is cocoa;
    Tea did for Johnson and the Chinamen:
When 'Dulce est desipere in loco'
    Was written, real Falernian winged the pen.

When a rapt audience has encored 'Fra Poco'
  Or 'Casta Diva', I have heard that then
The Prima Donna, smiling herself out,
Recruits her flagging powers with bottled stout.

But what is coffee, but a noxious berry,
  Born to keep used-up Londoners awake?
What is Falernian, what is Port or Sherry,
  But vile concoctions to make dull heads ache?
Nay stout itself – (though good with oysters, very) –
  Is not a thing your reading man should take.
He that would shine, and petrify his tutor,
Should drink draught Allsopp in its 'native pewter'.

But hark! a sound is stealing on my ear –
  A soft and silvery sound – I know it well.
Its tinkling tells me that a time is near
  Precious to me – it is the Dinner Bell.
O blessed Bell! Thou bringest beef and beer,
  Thou bringest good things more than tongue may tell:
Seared is, of course, my heart – but unsubdued
Is, and shall be, my appetite for food.

I go. Untaught and feeble is my pen:
  But on one statement I may safely venture:
That few of our most highly gifted men
  Have more appreciation of the trencher.
I go. One pound of British beef, and then
  What Mr Swiveller called a 'modest quencher';
That home-returning, I may 'soothly say',
'Fate cannot touch me: I have dined to-day.'

                              C. S. CALVERLEY

Ode to Tobacco

Thou who, when fears attack,
Bidst them avaunt, and Black
Care, at the horseman's back
    Perching, unseatest;
Sweet, when the morn is gray;
Sweet, when they've cleared away
Lunch; and at close of day
    Possibly sweetest:

I have a liking old
For thee, though manifold
Stories, I know, are told,
    Not to thy credit;
How one (or two at most)
Drops make a cat a ghost –
Useless, except to roast –
    Doctors have said it:

How they who use fusees
All grow by slow degrees
Brainless as chimpanzees,
    Meagre as lizards:
Go mad, and beat their wives;
Plunge (after shocking lives)
Razors and carving knives
    Into their gizzards.

Confound such knavish tricks!
Yet know I five or six
Smokers who freely mix
    Still with their neighbours;
Jones – (who, I'm glad to say,
Asked leave of Mrs J.) –

Daily absorbs a clay
    After his labours.

Cats may have had their goose
Cooked by tobacco-juice;
Still why deny its use
    Thoughtfully taken?
We're not as tabbies are:
Smith, take a fresh cigar!
Jones, the tobacco-jar!
    Here's to thee, Bacon!

C. S. CALVERLEY

Lines on Hearing the Organ

Grinder, who serenely grindest
    At my door the Hundredth Psalm,
Till thou ultimately findest
    Pence in thy unwashen palm:

Grinder, jocund-hearted Grinder,
    Near whom Barbary's nimble son,
Poised with skill upon his hinder
    Paws, accepts the proffered bun:

Dearly do I love thy grinding;
    Joy to meet thee on thy road
Where thou prowlest through the blinding
    Dust with that stupendous load,

'Neath the baleful star of Sirius,
    When the postmen slowlier jog,
And the ox becomes delirious,
    And the muzzle decks the dog.

Tell me by what art thou bindest
    On thy feet those ancient shoon:
Tell me, Grinder, if thou grindest
    Always, always out of tune.

Tell me if, as thou art buckling
    On thy straps with eager claws,
Thou forecastest, inly chuckling,
    All the rage that thou wilt cause.

Tell me if at all thou mindest
    When folks flee, as if on wings,
From thee as at ease thou grindest:
    Tell me fifty thousand things.

Grinder, gentle-hearted Grinder!
    Ruffians who lead evil lives,
Soothed by thy sweet strains, are kinder
    To their bullocks and their wives:

Children, when they see thy supple
    Form approach, are out like shots;
Half-a-bar sets several couple
    Waltzing in convenient spots;

Not with clumsy Jacks or Georges:
    Unprofaned by grasp of man
Maidens speed those simple orgies,
    Betsey Jane with Betsey Ann.

As they love thee in St Giles's
    Thou art loved in Grosvenor Square:
None of those engaging smiles is
    Unreciprocated there.

Often, ere yet thou hast hammer'd
   Through thy four delicious airs,
Coins are flung thee by enamour'd
   Housemaids upon area stairs:

E'en the ambrosial-whisker'd flunkey
   Eyes thy boots and thine unkempt
Beard and melancholy monkey
   More in pity than contempt.

Far from England, in the sunny
   South, where Arno leaps in foam,
Thou wast rear'd, till lack of money
   Drew thee from thy vineclad home:

And thy mate, the sinewy Jocko,
   From Brazil or Afric came,
Land of simoom and sirocco —
   And he seems extremely tame.

There he quaff'd the undefilèd
   Spring, or hung with apelike glee
By his teeth or tail or eyelid,
   To the slippery mango-tree:

There he woo'd and won a dusky
   Bride, of instincts like his own;
Talk'd of love till he was husky
   In a tongue to us unknown:

Side by side 'twas theirs to ravage
   The potato ground, or cut
Down the unsuspecting savage
   With the well-aim'd cocoa-nut: —

Till the miscreant Stranger tore him
    Screaming from his blue-faced fair;
And they flung strange raiment o'er him,
    Raiment which he could not bear:

Sever'd from the pure embraces
    Of his children and his spouse,
He must ride fantastic races
    Mounted on reluctant sows:

But the heart of wistful Jocko
    Still was with his ancient flame
In the nutgroves of Morocco;
    Or if not it's all the same.

Grinder, winsome grinsome Grinder!
    They who see thee and whose soul
Melts not at thy charms, are blinder
    Than a trebly-bandaged mole:

They to whom thy curt (yet clever)
    Talk, thy music and thine ape,
Seem not to be joys for ever,
    Are but brutes in human shape.

'Tis not that thy mien is stately,
    'Tis not that thy tones are soft;
'Tis not that I care so greatly
    For the same thing play'd so oft:

But I've heard mankind abuse thee;
    And perhaps it's rather strange,
But I thought that I would choose thee
    For encomium, as a change.

C. S. CALVERLEY

Lovers, and a Reflexion

In moss-prankt dells which the sunbeams flatter
    (And heaven it knoweth what that may mean;
Meaning, however, is no great matter)
    Where woods are a-tremble, with rifts atween;

Thro' God's own heather we wonn'd together,
    I and my Willie (O love my love):
I need hardly remark it was glorious weather,
    And flitterbats waver'd alow, above:

Boats were curtseying, rising, bowing,
    (Boats in that climate are so polite),
And sands were a ribbon of green endowing,
    And O the sundazzle on bark and bight!

Thro' the rare red heather we danced together,
    (O love my Willie!) and smelt for flowers:
I must mention again it was gorgeous weather,
    Rhymes are so scarce in this world of ours: –

By rises that flush'd with their purple favours,
    Thro' becks that brattled o'er grasses sheen,
We walked and waded, we two young shavers,
    Thanking our stars we were both so green.

We journeyed in parallels, I and Willie,
    In fortunate parallels! Butterflies,
Hid in weltering shadows of daffodilly
    Or marjoram, kept making peacock eyes:

Songbirds darted about, some inky
    As coal, some snowy (I ween) as curds;

Or rosy as pinks, or as roses pinky –
　　They reck of no eerie To-come, those birds!

But they skim over bents which the millstream washes,
　　Or hang in the lift 'neath a white cloud's hem;
They need no parasols, no goloshes;
　　And good Mrs Trimmer she feedeth them.

Then we thrid God's cowslips (as erst His heather)
　　That endowed the wan grass with their golden blooms;
And snapt – (it was perfectly charming weather) –
　　Our fingers at Fate and her goddess-glooms:

And Willie 'gan sing (O, his notes were fluty;
　　Wafts fluttered them out to the white-wing'd sea) –
Something made up of rhymes that have done much duty,
　　Rhymes (better to put it) of 'ancientry':

Bowers of flowers encounter'd showers
　　In William's carol – (O love my Willie!)
Then he bade sorrow borrow from blithe to-morrow
　　I quite forget what – say a daffodilly:

A nest in a hollow, 'with buds to follow',
　　I think occurred next in his nimble strain;
And clay that was 'kneaden' of course in Eden –
　　A rhyme most novel, I do maintain:

Mists, bones, the singer himself, love-stories,
　　And all least furlable things got 'furled';
Not with any design to conceal their 'glories',
　　But simply and solely to rhyme with 'world'.

*

O if billows and pillows and hours and flowers,
　　And all the brave rhymes of an elder day,

Could be furled together, this genial weather,
 And carted, or carried on 'wafts' away,
Nor ever again trotted out – ah me!
How much fewer volumes of verse there'd be!

                              C. S. CALVERLEY

The Schoolmaster

ABROAD WITH HIS SON

O what harper could worthily harp it,
 Mine Edward! this wide-stretching wold
(Look out *wold*) with its wonderful carpet
 Of emerald, purple, and gold!
Look well at it – also look sharp, it
  Is getting so cold.

The purple is heather (*erica*);
 The yellow, gorse – call'd sometimes 'whin'.
Cruel boys on its prickles might spike a
 Green beetle as if on a pin.
You may roll in it, if you would like a
  Few holes in your skin.

You wouldn't? Then think of how kind you
 Should be to the insects who crave
Your compassion – and then, look behind you
 At yon barley-ears! Don't they look brave
As they undulate (*undulate*, mind you,
  From *unda*, *a wave*).

The noise of those sheep-bells, how faint it
 Sounds here – (on account of our height)!

And this hillock itself – who could paint it,
  With its changes of shadow and light?
Is it not – (never, Eddy, say 'ain't it') –
  A marvellous sight?

Then yon desolate eerie morasses,
  The haunts of the snipe and the hern –
(I shall question the two upper classes
  On *aquatiles*, when we return) –
Why, I see on them absolute masses
  Of *filix* or fern.

How it interests e'en a beginner
  (Or *tiro*) like dear little Ned!
Is he listening? As I am a sinner
  He's asleep – he is wagging his head
Wake up! I'll go home to my dinner,
  And you to your bed.

The boundless ineffable prairie;
  The splendour of mountain and lake
With their hues that seem ever to vary;
  The mighty pine-forests which shake
In the wind, and in which the unwary
  May tread on a snake;

And this wold with its heathery garment
  Are themes undeniably great.
But – although there is not any harm in't –
  It's perhaps little good to dilate
On their charms to a dull little varmint
  Of seven or eight.

C. S. CALVERLEY

A Woice of the Wicious

'Ere, Bill, you listen, while I tell
'Ow I've just done the Mission: well,
The blokes all come, and fust some swell
      As seemed important;

Ses he: – 'Dear lads, what's vicked bin,
We vish to rexcue you from sin
And see you earnin' honest tin,
      If you'll allow us.'

And then some old 'un speaks genteel
And axes 'ow your innuds feel,
And 'ow yer fust was drew to steal,
      And then you blubs.

They called it 'druv', they did, by gum!
I dayn't say 'twarn't, but kept quite mum;
But all their talk's so precious rum,
      A kid must veep or laugh.

In course a vise un veeps – dayn't I?
And then says they: – 'My lad, don't cry –
We'll see to you.' Ses I: – 'O why
      Veren't you my parients?'

That paid, my cockie, just a few,
They stared at me a minute or two,
Then chummed together, and I knew
      I'd took their vind.

My heyes and limbs, what game it **is**
To stand and pull a Solomon phiz,

And bust to make the blubber rig,
        And come the penitent.

So now I specs to get repweave,
A stunnin' character, and I b'lieve
Not three week more afore I leave
        This Penny Stenchery.

But spose them buffers (oh my vig!)
'Adnt come and I 'adnt played this rig,
Why, I shouldn't get a horse and gig
        If I lived to ninety.

A steady cove is all my heye,
D'ye think I'd go to starve and cry
' 'Ot taters', when i' this-un's I
        Becomes so interestin'

There is some folks as takes it meek
And starve theirselves to 'scape the Beak,
While us 'deluded' kids are slick
        As Bottomuppermosts.

Now Bill, my say is this (which I'm
On Fortin's path) recelect this rhyme,
That 'Honesty's the thief of time' –
        You mark my wurds.

                             C. P.

On Mary Ann Lowder

Here lies the body of Mary Ann Lowder,
She burst while drinking a seidlitz powder.
Called from this world to her heavenly rest,
She should have waited till it effervesced.

                         ANON.

In Memoriam Examinatoris Cuiusdam

Lo, where yon undistinguished grave
   Erects its grassy pile on
One who to all Experience gave
   An Alpha or Epsilon.

The world and eke the world's content,
   And all therein that passes,
With marks numerical (per cent)
   He did dispose in classes:

Not his to ape the critic crew
   Which vulgarly appraises
The Good, the Beautiful, the True
   In literary phrases:

He did his estimate express
   In terms precise and weighty, –
And Vice got 25 (or less),
   While Virtue rose to 80.

Now hath he closed his earthly lot
   All in his final haven, –
(And be the stone that marks the spot
   On one side only graven);[1]

Bring papers on his grave to strew
   Amid the grass and clover,
And plant thereby that pencil blue
   Wherewith he looked them over!

1. Candidates in University examinations are requested to write 'on one side of their paper only'.

There freed from every human ill
    And fleshly trammels gross, he
Lies in his resting place until
    The final Viva Voce:

So let him rest till crack of doom,
    Of mortal tasks aweary, –
And nothing write upon his tomb
    Save β — (?).

A. D. GODLEY

The Bards

My aged friend, Miss Wilkinson,
    Whose mother was a Lambe,
Saw Wordsworth once, and Coleridge, too,
    One morning in her 'pram'.[1]

Birdlike the bards stooped over her
    Like fledgling in a nest;
And Wordsworth said, 'Thou harmless babe!'
    And Coleridge was impressed.

The pretty thing gazed up and smiled,
    And softly murmured, 'Coo!'
William was then aged sixty-four
    And Samuel sixty-two.

WALTER DE LA MARE

1. This was a three wheeled vehicle
    Of iron and of wood;
  It had a leather apron,
    But it hadn't any hood.

Culture in the Slums

BALLADE

I often does a quiet read
    At Booty Shelly's poetry;
I thinks that Swinburne at a screed
    Is really almost too too fly;
    At Signor Vagna's harmony
I likes a merry little flutter;
    I've had at Pater many a shy;
In fact, my form's the Bloomin' Utter.

My mark's a tidy little feed,
    And 'Enery Irving's gallery,
To see old 'Amlick do a bleed,
    And Ellen Terry on the die,
    Or Frankey's ghostes at hi-spy,
And parties carried on a shutter.
    Them vulgar Coupeaus is my eye!
In fact, my form's the Bloomin' Utter.

The Grosvenor's nuts — it is, indeed!
    I goes for 'Olman 'Unt like pie.
It's equal to a friendly lead
    To see B. Jones's judes go by.
    Stanhope he make me fit to cry.
Whistler he makes me melt like butter.
    Strudwick he makes me flash my cly —
In fact, my form's the Bloomin' Utter.

ENVOY

I'm on for any Art that's 'Igh;
I talks as quiet as I can splutter;

I keeps a Dado on the sly;
In fact, my form's the Bloomin' Utter.

W. E. HENLEY

The Lady with Technique

As I was letting down my hair
I met a guy who didn't care;
He didn't care again to-day –
I *love* 'em when they get that way!

HUGHES MEARNS

Frustrated Male

One night I met when stepping out
A gal who wasn't thereabout;
I said, '*Hel*-lo! And how are *you*!'
She didn't say; so I never knew.

HUGHES MEARNS

Reveille

The porter shouted, 'Syracuse!'
And shook me hard and cried, 'Excuse,
Ef you wa'n't goin' to La Cross
This is where I'd wake you, Boss!'

HUGHES MEARNS

The Practical Joker

Oh, what a fund of joy jocund lies hid in harmless hoaxes!
   What keen enjoyment springs
   From cheap and simple things!
What deep delight from sources trite inventive humour coaxes,
   That pain and trouble brew
   For every one but you!
Gunpowder placed inside its waist improves a mild Havana,
   Its unexpected flash
   Burns eyebrows and moustache.
When people dine no kind of wine beats ipecacuanha,
   But common sense suggests
   You keep it for your guests –
Then naught annoys the organ boys like throwing red hot coppers.
   And much amusement bides
   In common butter slides;
And stringy snares across the stairs cause unexpected croppers.
   Coal scuttles, recollect,
   Produce the same effect.
    A man possessed
     Of common sense
    Need not invest
     At great expense –
    It does not call
     For pocket deep,
    These jokes are all
     Extremely cheap.
If you commence with eighteenpence – it's all you'll have to pay;
You may command a pleasant and a most instructive day.

A good spring gun breeds endless fun, and makes men jump like
   rockets –
   And turnip heads on posts
   Make very decent ghosts.

Then hornets sting like anything, when placed in waistcoat
    pockets –
        Burnt cork and walnut juice
        Are not without their use.
No fun compares with easy chairs whose seats are stuffed with
    needles –
        Live shrimps their patience tax
        When put down people's backs.
Surprising, too, what one can do with a pint of fat black beetles –
        And treacle on a chair
        Will make a Quaker swear!
          Then sharp tin tacks
            And pocket squirts –
          And cobbler's wax
            For ladies' skirts –
          And slimy slugs
            On bedroom floors –
          And water jugs
            On open doors –
Prepared with these cheap properties, amusing tricks to play
Upon a friend a man may spend a most delightful day.

SIR W. S. GILBERT

Nightmare

When you're lying awake with a dismal headache, and repose is
    taboo'd by anxiety,
I conceive you may use any language you choose to indulge in,
    without impropriety;
For your brain is on fire – the bedclothes conspire of usual slumber
    to plunder you:
First your counterpane goes, and uncovers your toes, and your
    sheet slips demurely from under you;
Then the blanketing tickles – you feel like mixed pickles – so
    terribly sharp is the pricking,

And you're hot, and you're cross, and you tumble and toss till
　　there's nothing 'twixt you and the ticking.

Then the bedclothes all creep to the ground in a heap, and you pick
　　'em all up in a tangle;

Next your pillow resigns and politely declines to remain at its usual
　　angle!

Well, you get some repose in the form of a doze, with hot eye-balls,
　　and head ever aching,

But your slumbering teems with such horrible dreams that you'd
　　very much better be waking;

For you dream you are crossing the Channel, and tossing about in
　　a steamer from Harwich –

Which is something between a large bathing machine and a very
　　small second-class carriage –

And you're giving a treat (penny ice and cold meat) to a party of
　　friends and relations –

They're a ravenous horde – and they all came on board at Sloane
　　Square and South Kensington Stations.

And bound on that journey you find your attorney (who started
　　that morning from Devon);

He's a bit undersized, and you don't feel surprised when he tells
　　you he's only eleven.

Well, you're driving like mad with this singular lad (by-the-bye the
　　ship's now a four-wheeler),

And you're playing round games, and he calls you bad names when
　　you tell him that 'ties pay the dealer'.

But this you can't stand, so you throw up your hand, and you find
　　you're as cold as an icicle,

In your shirt and your socks (the black silk with gold clocks),
　　crossing Salisbury Plain on a bicycle:

And he and the crew are on bicycles too – which they've somehow
　　or other invested in –

And he's telling the tars, all the particulars of a company he's
　　interested in –

It's a scheme of devices, to get at low prices, all goods from cough
　　mixtures to cables

(Which tickled the sailors) by treating retailers, as though they
    were all vege*t*ables –

You get a good spadesman to plant a small tradesman (first take off
    his boots with a boot-tree),

And his legs will take root, and his fingers will shoot, and they'll
    blossom and bud like a fruit-tree –

From the greengrocer tree to get grapes and green pea, cauliflower,
    pineapple, and cranberries,

While the pastrycook plant, cherry brandy will grant, apple puffs,
    and three-corners, and banberries –

The shares are a penny, and ever so many are taken by
    ROTHSCHILD and BARING,

And just as a few are allotted to you, you awake with a shudder
    despairing –

You're a regular wreck, with a crick in your neck, and no wonder
    you snore, for your head's on the floor, and you've needles
    and pins from your soles to your shins, and your flesh is
    a-creep for your left leg's asleep, and you've cramp in your
    toes, and a fly on your nose, and some fluff in your lung,
    and a feverish tongue, and a thirst that's intense, and a
    general sense that you haven't been sleeping in clover;

But the darkness has passed, and it's daylight at last, and the night
    has been long – ditto ditto my song – and thank goodness
    they're both of them over!

SIR W. S. GILBERT

The Young Lady from Wantage

There was a young lady from Wantage
Of whom the town clerk took advantage.
    Said the borough surveyor:
    'Indeed you must pay 'er.
You've totally altered her frontage.'

ANON.

Wine and Water

Old Noah he had an ostrich farm and fowls on the largest scale,
He ate his egg with a ladle in an egg-cup big as a pail,
And the soup he took was Elephant Soup and the fish he took was
        Whale,
But they all were small to the cellar he took when he set out to sail,
And Noah he often said to his wife when he sat down to dine,
'I don't care where the water goes if it doesn't get into the wine.'

The cataract of the cliff of heaven fell blinding off the brink
As if it would wash the stars away as suds go down a sink,
The seven heavens came roaring down for the throats of hell to
        drink,
And Noah he cocked his eye and said, 'It looks like rain, I think.
The water has drowned the Matterhorn as deep as a Mendip mine,
But I don't care where the water goes if it doesn't get into the wine.'

But Noah he sinned, and we have sinned; on tipsy feet we trod,
Till a great big black teetotaller was sent for us for a rod,
And you can't get wine at a P.S.A., or chapel, or Eisteddfod,
For the Curse of Water has come again because of the wrath of God,
And water is on the Bishop's board and the Higher Thinker's
        shrine,
But I don't care where the water goes if it doesn't get into the wine.

G. K. CHESTERTON

Ballade of an Anti-Puritan

They spoke of Progress spiring round,
Of Light and Mrs Humphry Ward –
It is not true to say I frowned,
Or ran about the room and roared;

I might have simply sat and snored –
I rose politely in the club
And said, 'I feel a little bored;
Will someone take me to a pub?'

The new world's wisest did surround
Me; and it pains me to record
I did not think their views profound,
Or their conclusions well assured;
The simple life I can't afford,
Besides, I do not like the grub –
I want a mash and sausage, 'scored' –
Will someone take me to a pub?

I know where Men can still be found,
Anger and clamorous accord,
And virtues growing from the ground,
And fellowship of beer and board,
And song, that is a sturdy cord,
And hope, that is a hardy shrub,
And goodness, that is God's last word –
Will someone take me to a pub?

ENVOI

Prince, Bayard would have smashed his sword
To see the sort of knights you dub –
Is that the last of them – O Lord!
Will someone take me to a pub?

G. K. CHESTERTON

Ballade of Suicide

The gallows in my garden, people say,
Is new and neat and adequately tall.

I tie the noose on in a knowing way
As one that knots his necktie for a ball;
But just as all the neighbours – on the wall –
Are drawing a long breath to shout 'Hurray!'
The strangest whim has seized me . . . After all
I think I will not hang myself to-day.

To-morrow is the time I get my pay –
My uncle's sword is hanging in the hall –
I see a little cloud all pink and grey –
Perhaps the rector's mother will not call –
I fancy that I heard from Mr Gall
That mushrooms could be cooked another way –
I never read the works of Juvenal –
I think I will not hang myself to-day.

The world will have another washing day;
The decadents decay; the pedants pall;
And H. G. Wells has found that children play,
And Bernard Shaw discovered that they squall;
Rationalists are growing rational –
And through thick woods one finds a stream astray,
So secret that the very sky seems small –
I think I will not hang myself to-day.

ENVOI

Prince, I can hear the trump of Germinal,
The tumbrils toiling up the terrible way;
Even to-day your royal head may fall –
I think I will not hang myself to-day.

G. K. CHESTERTON

Ballade of Vain Delight

Howling the chorus of a comic song
   I stagger home to bed at half-past three.
A spirited performance on the gong
   Brings down my maiden aunt in *robe de nuit.*
   She tells me she considers it to be
Her duty to inform me that Miss Bliss
   This morning saw me wink at Melanee.
What is the use of going on like this?

Alone I wander 'mid the giddy throng.
   Last Thursday evening, feeling like a spree
(Although my conscience told me it was wrong),
   I put some strychnine in my parents' tea.
   Alas! Alas! How well, too late, I see
My own improvidence and thoughtlessness!
   Who is there now to love and comfort me?
What is the use of going on like this?

I'm growing deaf. My lungs are far from strong.
   I stoop and shuffle like a chimpanzee.
My stories are interminably long.
   I laugh at them myself consumedly.
   I talk about my mother's pedigree.
I note a tendency to avarice.
   These are thy wages, O debauchery!
What is the use of going on like this?

ENVOI

   Prince, what is that you're hiding? Let me see.
A note from Mr Semitopolis!

He will be pleased to come and shoot, will he?
What is the use of going on like this?

E. C. BENTLEY

Ballade of Plain Common Sense

The croakers say that Mr Justice Peck
    Was briefless both as junior and K.C.
That nasty business of the altered cheque
    Was never quite hushed up, unhappily,
    But still, it was the Bench or bankruptcy;
Besides, the man was getting on in years,
    And nothing done for him. It had to be.
I simply wag my great, long, furry ears.

They say the Duke of Deal is wont to deck
    His forehead with a huge phylactery;
They say Sir Buckley Boldwood is a Czech,
    And Lord Fitz Waldemar a Portuguee;
    They say Lord Penge began in poverty
Outside Pompeii, selling souvenirs.
    I cannot think of any repartee,
I simply wag my great, long, furry ears.

They speak of England as a moral wreck,
    Stone-blind and deaf to all reality;
Her mind asleep, the usurer on her neck,
    Her God forgotten, and her history.
    They say, 'Shall these things perish utterly,
These that were England through the glorious years –
    Faith and green fields and honour and the sea?'
I simply wag my great, long, furry ears.

ENVOI

Prince, they deride your purse, your pedigree,
Your taste in Art, and wine, and clothes, and peers.
  Such things make no impression upon me;
I simply wag my great, long, furry ears.

E. C. BENTLEY

Student

While the Persians
Undoubtedly were given to
Several interesting perversions

I consider
The political customs of England
Were, in growth, far rapider.

GAVIN EWART

Ambitionist

I should like to see
Better become best;
I should like to see the savage
Wear both shirt and vest.

I should like to see
The Daily Press
Taking its cues
From the weekly reviews.

GAVIN EWART

The Schoolmaster Abroad

(The Steam Yacht 'Argonaut' was chartered from Messrs Perowne and Lunn
by a body of Public School Masters for the purpose of an educative visit to the
Levant.)

O 'Isles', as Byron said, 'of Greece!'
    For which the firm of Homer sang,
Especially that little piece
    Interpreted by Mr Lang;
Where the unblushing Sappho wrote
The hymns we hardly like to quote.

I cannot share his grave regret
    Who found your fame had been and gone;
There seems to be a future yet
    For Tenedos and Marathon,
Fresh glory gilds their deathless sun,
And this is due to Dr Lunn!

What though your harpers twang no more?
    What though your various lyres are dumb?
See where by Cirrha's sacred shore,
    Bold Argonauts, the Ushers come!
And bring their maps, and some their wives,
And at the vision Greece revives!

The Delphic oracles are off,
    But still the site is always there;
The fumes that made the Pythian cough
    Still permeate the conscious air;
Parnassus, of the arduous 'grade',
May still be climbed, with local aid.

Lunching upon the self-same rock
    Whence Xerxes viewed the wine-red frith,

They realize with vivid shock
    The teachings of 'the smaller Smith';
With bated breath they murmur – 'This
Is actually Salamis!'

They visit where Penelope
    Nightly unwove the work of day,
Staving her suitors off till he,
    Ulysses, let the long-bow play,
And in his brave grass-widow's breast
Forgot Calypso and the rest.

In Crete, where Theseus first embraced
    His Ariadne, they explore
(Just now authentically traced)
    The footprints of the minotaur,
And follow, to the maze's source,
The thread of some profound discourse.

That isle where Leto, sick with fright,
    So scandalized her mortal kin,
Where young Apollo, lord of light
    Commenced his progress as a twin –
Fair Delos, they shall get to know,
And Paros, where the marbles grow.

Not theirs the course of crude delight
    On which the common tourist wends;
From faith they move, by way of sight,
    To knowledge meant for noble ends,
'Twill be among their purest joys
To work it off upon the boys.

One hears the travelled teacher call
    Upon the Upper Fifth to note

(Touching the Spartan counter-wall)
    How great the lore of Mr Grote:
And tell them, 'His are just the views
I formed myself – at Syracuse!'

When Jones is at a loss to show
    Where certain islands ought to be,
How well to whack him hard and low,
    And say, 'The pain is worse for me.
To whom the Cyclades are quite
Familiar, like the Isle of Wight.'

And then the lecture after prep!
    The Magic Lantern's lurid slide!
The speaker pictured on the step
    Of some old shrine, with no inside,
Or groping on his reverent knees
For Eleusinian mysteries!

Hellas defunct? O say not so,
    When Public School-boys faint to hear
The tales of antique love or woe,
    Brought home and rendered strangely clear
With instantaneous Kodak shots
Secured by Ushers on the spots!

SIR OWEN SEAMAN

The Crimes of Lizzie Borden

Lizzie Borden with an axe,
Hit her father forty whacks.
When she saw what she had done,
She hit her mother forty-one.

ANON.

Ballade of Soporific Absorption

Ho! Ho! Yes! Yes! It's very all well,
　　You may drunk I am think, but I tell you I'm **not**,
I'm as sound as a fiddle and fit as a bell,
　　And stable quite ill to see what's what.
　　I under *do* stand you surprise a got
When I headed my smear with gooseberry jam:
　　And I've swallowed, I grant, a beer of lot –
But I'm not so think as you drunk I am.

Can I liquor my stand? Why, yes, like hell!
　　I care not how many a tossed I've pot,
I shall stralk quite weight and not yutter an ell,
　　My feech will not spalter the least little jot:
　　If you knownly had own! – well, I gave him a dot,
And I said to him, 'Sergeant, I'll come like a lamb –
　　The floor it seems like a storm in a yacht,
But I'm not so think as you drunk I am.'

For example, to prove it I'll tale you a tell –
　　I once knew a fellow named Apricot –
I'm sorry, I just chair over a fell –
　　A trifle – this chap, on a very day hot –
　　If I hadn't consumed that last whisky of tot! –
As I said now, this fellow, called Abraham –
　　Ah? One more? Since it's you! Just a do me will spot –
But I'm not so think as you drunk I am.

ENVOI

　　So, Prince, you suggest I've bolted my shot?
Well, like what you say, and soul your damn!
　　I'm an upple litset by the talk you rot –
But I'm not so think as you drunk I am.

SIR J. C. SQUIRE

In Committee

As the committee musters,
'Silence for Noisy, let Noisy orate.'
Noisy himself blusters,
Shouldering up, mounting the dais,
And baritonely opens the debate
With cream-bun fallacies
With semi-nudes of platitudes
And testamentary feuds
Rushed at a slap-stick rate
To a jangling end.
Immediately he
Begins again, pleads confidentially:
'Be grateful to your Noisy,
The old firm, your old friend –'
Whose bagpipe lungs express
Emphatic tunelessness.
How could we draft a fair report
Till all old Noisy's variants have been aired,
His complimentary discords paired,
Bellowing and squealing sort by sort
In Noah's Ark fashion;
Noisy's actual invalidation?

Applause. Up jumps Hasty. 'Excellent Hasty,
Three cheers for Hasty', sings out Hearty,
And is at once ejected
As he expected.
Hasty speaks. Hasty is diabetic,
Like a creature in spasms, pathetic, out of joint.
Stammers, cannot clear the point,
Only as he sinks back, from his seat
Spits out, 'Noisy you dog, you slug, you cheat.'
Enter the Chairman, late,

Gathers the threads of the debate,
Raps for order,
'Ragman, will you speak next, sir?'
Ragman pulls out his latest clippings,
Potsherds, tags of talk, flint chippings,
Quotations happy and miserable,
Various careless ologies, half a skull,
Commonplace books, blue books, cook books,
And artificial flies with tangled hooks.
'All genuine,' lamely says Ragman,
'Draw your own deductions, gentlemen,
I offer nothing.'

Critic crosses the floor, snuffling.
Draws casually from Ragman's bag
Two judgements, a fossil, a rag, a thread,
Compares them outspread,
'Here Noisy cheated, as Hasty said,
Though not as Hasty meant.
Use your discernment.
These objects prove both speakers lied:
One side first, then the other side.
    We can only say this much: —
So and So clearly is not such and such.
And the point is . . .' Critic wrinkles his nose.
'Use your discernment.'

Re-enter Hearty, enthusiastically repentant,
Cries 'Order, Order!' Uproar.
Chairman raps, is impotent.
Synthesis smoking in a corner
Groans, pulls himself together,
Holds his hand up, takes the floor,
'Gentleman, only a half-hour more
And nothing done. What's to be blamed?

No, no. Let us agree
First, that the motion's wrongly framed,
Two senses are confused, indeed three,
Next, the procedure's upside down.
Pray, Mr Chairman, Mr Secretary . . .
Let us hear Pro and Con
On the reconstituted motion.'

Pro and Con speak. Noisy makes no objection,
Busy recalling his oration
For instant publication.
Hasty makes no objection,
Busy clicking the blind cords up and down,
Nor Ragman (Ragman consults a Hebrew Lexicon),
Nor Critic (Critic drums with a pencil on the table),
Nor Hearty (Hearty is affable
In bubbling praise of Ragman's knowledge).
Synthesis sums up, nerves on edge.
Critic amends a small detail.
Synthesis accepts it, not too proud.
Chairman reads the draft-report aloud,
'Resolved that this day fortnight without fail . . .'

All vote, all approve
With show of brotherly love,
And the clock strikes, just in time.
Hearty proposes in pun-strewn rhyme
A vote of thanks to all the officers.
Cheers drown Hasty's angry bark.
Noisy begins: 'Gentlemen and Philosophers . . .'
Critic hums: 'Not too ill a morning's work.'
Ragman's on all fours after scraps and crumbs.
Chairman turns out the gas: 'Come, Ragman!' Ragman comes;
Synthesis left sitting in the dark:
'I shall resign to-morrow, why stay

Flattered as indispensable
By this old rabble,
Not indispensable: and going grey?'

ROBERT GRAVES

«¡Wellcome, to the Caves of Arta!»

'They are hollowed out in the see-coast at the muncipal terminal of Capdepeı
at nine kilometer from the town of Arta in the Island of Mallorca, with a
suporizing infinity of graceful colums of 21 meter and by downward, which
prives the spectator of all animacion and plunges in dumbness. The way going
is very picturesque, serpentine between style mountains, til the arrival at the
esplanade of the vallee called «The Spider». There are good enlacements of the
railroad with autobuses of excursion, many days of the week, today actually
Wednesday and Satturday. Since many centuries renown foreing visitors have
explored them and wrote their elegy about, included Nort-American
geoglogues.' [From a tourist guide.]

Such subtile filigranity and nobless of construccion
    Here fraternise in harmony, that respiracion stops.
While all admit thier impotence (though autors most formidable)
    To sing in words the excellence of Nature's underprops,
Yet stalactite and stalagmite together with dumb language
    Make hymnes to God wich celebrate the stregnth of water drops.

¿You, also, are you capable to make precise in idiom
    Consideracions magic of ilusions very wide?
Already in the Vestibule of these Grand Caves of Arta
    The spirit of the human verb is darked and stupefyed;
So humildy you trespass trough the forest of the colums
    And listen to the grandess explicated by the guide.

From darkness into darkness, but at measure, now descending
    You remark with what esxactitude he designates each bent:
«The Saloon of Thousand Banners», or «The Tumba of Napoleon»,
    «The Grotto of the Rosary», «The Club», «The Camping Tent»,

And at «Cavern of the Organs» there are knocking strange
    formacions
    Wich give a nois particular pervoking wonderment.

¡Too far do not adventure, sir! For, further as you wander,
    The every of the stalactites will make you stop and stay.
Grand peril amenaces now, your nostrills aprehending
    An odour least delicious of lamentable decay.
It is some poor touristers, in the depth of obscure cristal,
    Wich deceased of thier emocion on a past excursion day.

ROBERT GRAVES

The Board Meets

The table's long and gleaming
With pads of virgin white,
And the men who are gathered about the board
Are serpentine-fronted and self-assured,
And frequently murmur: 'Quite!'

'Quite' is the symbol of wisdom
'Quite' is the word of power,
And fruity and rich are the tones in which
It is uttered hour by hour.

Clamouring 'quite' as a chorus,
The quorum records its vote,
And the chairman's smile and his store of guile
Have preserved an agreeable note,
    Quite! Quite!
And a paying idea's afloat.

JOHN GLOAG

Poems in Praise of Practically Nothing

FIRST SERIES

You're kind to women, children, worms;
You speak of God in the highest terms;
You help spell words like 'tetrahedral',
You show respect for a Cathedral;
You're sweet and gentle as a mouse is:
(Wives should behave so to their spouses!)
Though women tempt you more than plenty,
Your rate is half a girl in twenty.
In short, from grace you never fell yet –
And what do you get? On all sides hell yet!

You take a bath, and sit there bathing
In water cold, in water scathing;
You scrub till you're sans an epidermis
And feel like a regular bathing Hermes.
You do not waste a single minute;
The tub shows how you worked while in it;
You dry, and do some honest rooting
For such remarkable abluting.
Well, a day goes by, or ten, or thirty,
And what thanks do you get? You're just as dirty!

You meet a girl and you surrender;
Though God knows why, you're kind and tender;
You're husband, lover, sister, brother,
Companion, banker, father, mother;
You try your best to be worthy of her;
You make mistakes, but she knows you love her;
You're hers completely, and you show it.
And what thanks do you get? The gate – I know it!

You're a good girl; you're grey with virtue;
The very thought of a misstep hurts you;
You know that honour must be hoarded
Against the day when it is rewarded.
You see a girl who's all men's vassal
Marry a duke in his own castle;
You see another who can't say 'No, sir'
Capture at least a wholesale grocer.
But you never let your thoughts grow sordid:
You know in your heart you'll be rewarded.
Well, the years go by, like Queens and roses,
The way they did in the time of Moses,
And what do you get? False teeth, a doorman,
A complex, or assistant foreman!

You hire a cook, but she can't cook yet;
You teach her by candle, bell, and book yet;
You show her, as if she were in her cradle,
To-day the soup, to-morrow a ladle.
Well, she doesn't learn, so although you need her
You decide that somebody else should feed her.
But you're kind by birth; you hate to fire her –
To tell a woman you don't require her.
So you wait and wait, and before you do it,
What thanks do you get? She beats you to it!

Poems in Praise of Practically Nothing

SECOND SERIES

You buy some flowers for your table;
You tend them tenderly as you're able;
You fetch them water from hither and thither –
What thanks do you get for it all? They wither.

Only the wholesomest foods you eat;
You lave and you lave from your head to your feet;
The earth is not steadier on its axis
Than you in the matter of prophylaxis;
You go to bed early, and early you rise;
You scrub your teeth and you scour your eyes —
What thanks do you get for it all? Nephritis,
Pneumonia, appendicitis,
Renal calculus and gastritis.

You get a girl; and you say you love her;
You pan the comparative stars above her;
You roast the comparative roses below her;
You throw the bull that you'll never throw her —
What thanks do you get? The very first whozis
Who tips his mitt, with him she vamooses.

You buy yourself a new suit of clothes;
The care you give it, God only knows;
The material, of course, is the very best yet;
You get it pressed and pressed and pressed yet;
You keep it free from specks so tiny —
What thanks do you get? The pants get shiny.

You practise every possible virtue;
You hurt not a soul, while others hurt you;
You fetch and carry like a market basket;
What thanks do you get for it? Me don't ask it!

You leap out of bed; you start to get ready;
You dress and you dress till you feel unsteady;
Hours go by, and you're still busy
Putting on clothes, till your brain is dizzy.

Do you flinch, do you quit, do you go out naked? –
The least little button, you don't forsake it.
What thanks do you get? Well, for all this mess, yet
When night comes around you've got to undress yet.

SAMUEL HOFFENSTEIN

Family Court

One would be in less danger
From the wiles of the stranger
If one's own kin and kith
Were more fun to be with.

OGDEN NASH

A Bas Ben Adhem

My fellow man I do not care for.
I often ask me, What's he there for?
The only answer I can find
Is, Reproduction of his kind.

OGDEN NASH

Lather as You Go

Beneath this slab
John Brown is stowed.
He watched the ads
And not the road.

OGDEN NASH

Pot Pourri from a Surrey Garden

Miles of pram in the wind and Pam in the gorse track,
    Coco-nut smell of the broom and a packet of Weights
Press'd in the sand. The thud of a hoof on a horse track –
A horse-riding horse for a horse-track –
        Conifer county of Surrey approached
Through remarkable wrought-iron gates.

Over your boundary now, I wash my face in a bird-bath,
    Then which path shall I take? That over there by the pram?
Down by the pond? or else, shall I take the slippery third path,
        Trodden away with gymn. shoes,
        Beautiful fir-dry alley that leads
To the bountiful body of Pam?

Pam, I adore you, Pam, you great big mountainous sports girl,
    Whizzing them over the net, full of the strength of five;
That old Malvernian brother, you zephyr and khaki shorts girl,
        Although he's playing for Woking,
Can't stand up to your wonderful backhand drive.

See the strength of her arm, as firm and hairy as Hendren's;
    See the size of her thighs, the pout of her lips as, cross,
And full of a pent-up strength, she swipes at the rhododendrons,
        Lucky the rhododendrons,
        And flings her arrogant love-lock
Back with a petulant toss.

Over the redolent pinewoods, in at the bathroom casement,
    One fine Saturday, Windlesham bells shall call
Up the Butterfield aisle rich with Gothic enlacement,
        Licensed now for embracement,
Pam and I, as the organ
    Thunders over you all.

JOHN BETJEMAN

The Archaeological Picnic

In this high pasturage, the Blunden time,
    With Lady's Finger, Smokewort, Lovers' Loss,
And lin-lan-lone a Tennysonian chime
    Stirring the sorrel and the gold-starred moss,
    Cool is the chancel, bright the Altar cross.

Drink, Mary, drink your fizzy lemonade
    And leave the king-cups. Take your grey felt hat;
Here where the low side window lends a shade,
    There, where the key lies underneath the mat
    The rude forefathers of the hamlet sat.

Sweet smell of cerements and cold wet stones,
    Hassock and cassock, paraffin and pew,
Green in a light which that sublime Burne-Jones
    White-hot and wondering from the glass kiln drew
    Gleams and re-gleams the Trans arcade anew.

So stand you waiting, freckled innocence!
    For me the squinch and squint and Trans arcade:
For you, where meadow grass is evidence
    With flattened pattern by our picnic made,
    One bottle more of fizzy lemonade.

                                        JOHN BETJEMAN

Song of the Open Road

I think that I shall never see
A billboard lovely as a tree.
Perhaps unless the billboards fall,
I'll never see a tree at all.

                            OGDEN NASH

The Sniffle

In spite of her sniffle
Isabel's chiffle.
Some girls with a sniffle
Would be weepy and tiffle;
They would look awful,
Like a rained-on waffle,
But Isabel's chiffle
In spite of her sniffle.
Her nose is more red
With a cold in her head,
But then, to be sure,
Her eyes are bluer.
Some girls with a snuffle,
Their tempers are uffle.
But when Isabel's snivelly
She's snivelly civilly,
And when she's snuffly
She's perfectly luffly.

OGDEN NASH

Lines on Facing Forty

I have a bone to pick with fate,
Come here and tell me, girlie,
Do you think my mind is maturing late,
Or simply rotted early?

OGDEN NASH

PROTESTS
AND EXPOSTULATIONS

A Curse on the Cat

O cat of churlish kind,
The fiend was in thy mind
When thou my bird untwin'd! [1]
I would thou hadst been blind!
The leopards savage,
The lions in their rage
Might catch thee in their paws,
And gnaw thee in their jaws!
The serpents of Libany
Might sting thee venomously!
The dragons with their tongues
Might poison thy liver and lungs!
The manticors [2] of the mountains
Might feed upon thy brains!

JOHN SKELTON

Against Garnesche

When ye were younger of age
Ye were a kitchen page,
A dish-washer, a drivell, [3]
In the pot your nose did snivell;
Ye fried and ye broiled,
Ye roasted and ye boiled
Ye roasted, like a fon, [4]
A goose with the feet upon;
Ye sluffered up souce [5]
In my lady Brewse's house.

1. destroyed.   2. human-headed dragons.
   3. drudge.   4. fool.   5. tripes.

F 2

Whereto should I write
Of such a greasy Knight?
A bawdy dish-clout
That bringeth the world about
With hafting and with polling [1]
With lying and controlling.

JOHN SKELTON

Doctors of the Vintrie

A little rag of rhetoric,
A less lump of logic,
A piece or a patch of philosophy,
Then forthwith by and by
They tumble so in theology,
Drowned in dregs of divinity,
That they judge themselves to be
Doctors of the chair in the Vintrie
At the Three Cranes . . .

JOHN SKELTON

On my Joyful Departure from the City of Cologne

As I am a Rhymer
And now at least a merry one,
Mr Mum's Rudesheimer
And the church of St Geryon
Are the two things alone
That deserve to be known
In the body-and-soul-stinking town of Cologne.

S. T. COLERIDGE

1. deceiving and stealing.

Mrs Frances Harris's Petition, 1699

To their Excellencies the Lords Justices of Ireland,
The humble petition of Frances Harris,
Who must starve and die a maid if it miscarries;
Humbly sheweth that I went to warm myself in Lady Betty's
    chamber because I was cold;
And I had in a purse seven pounds, four shillings and sixpence,
    (besides farthings) in money and gold;
So because I had been buying things for my Lady last night,
I was resolved to tell my money, to see if it was right.
For, you must know, because my trunk has a very bad lock,
Therefore all the money I have, which, God knows, is a very small
    stock,
I keep in my pocket, ty'd about my middle, next my smock.
So when I went to put up my purse, as God would have it, my
    smock was unript,
And instead of putting it into my pocket, down it slipt;
Then the bell rung, and I went down to put my lady to bed;
And, God knows, I thought my money was as safe as my maiden-
    head.
So, when I came up again, I found my pocket feel very light;
But when I search'd, and missed my purse, Lord! I thought I
    should have sunk outright.
'Lord, Madam,' says Mary, 'how d'ye do?' 'Indeed,' says I, 'never
    worse:
But pray, Mary, can you tell what I have done with my purse?'
'Lord help me,' says Mary, 'I never stirr'd out of this place!'
'Nay,' said I, 'I had it in Lady Betty's chamber, that's a plain
    case.'
So Mary got me to bed, and cover'd me up warm:
However, she stole away my garters, that I might do myself no
    harm.
So I tumbled and toss'd all night, as you may very well think.
But hardly ever set my eyes together, or slept a wink

So I was a-dream'd, methought, that I went and search'd the folkes
    round,
And in a corner of Mrs Dukes's box, ty'd in a rag, the money was
    found.
So next morning we told Whittle, and he fell a swearing:
Then my dame Wadgar came, and she, you know, is thick of
    hearing.
'Dame,' said I, as loud as I could bawl, 'do you know what a loss
    I have had?'
'Nay,' says she, 'my Lord Colway's folks are all very sad:
For my Lord Dromedary comes a Tuesday without fail.'
'Pugh,' said I, 'but that's not the business that I ail.'
Says Cary, says he, 'I have been a servant this five and twenty years
    come spring,
And in all the places I lived I never heard of such a thing.'
'Yes,' says the steward, 'I remember when I was at my Lord
    Shrewsbury's
Such a thing as this happen'd, just about the time of *gooseberries*.'
So I went to the party suspected, and I found her full of grief:
(Now, you must know, of all things in the world I hate a thief)
However, I was resolved to bring the discourse slyly about:
'Mrs Duke,' said I, 'here's an ugly accident has happened out:
'Tis not that I value the money three ships of a louse:
But the thing I stand upon is the credit of the house.
'Tis true, seven pounds, four shillings and sixpence makes a great
    hole in my wages:
Besides, as they say, service is no inheritance in these ages.
Now, Mrs Duke, you know, and everybody understands,
That though 'tis hard to judge, yet money can't go without hands.'
'The devil take me!' said she (blessing herself) 'if ever I saw't!'
So she roar'd like a bedlam, as thof I had call'd her all to naught.
So, you know, what could I say to her any more?
I e'en left her, and came away as wise as I was before.
Well; but then they would have had me gone to the cunning man:
'No,' said I, ''tis the same thing, the CHAPLAIN will be here anon.'
So the Chaplain came in. Now the servants say he is my sweetheart,

Because he's always in my chamber, and I always take his part.
So, as the *devil* would have it, before I was aware, out I blunder'd,
'*Parson*,' said I, 'can you cast a *nativity*, when a body's plunder'd?'
(Now you must know, he hates to be call'd Parson, like the *devil!*)
'Truly,' says he, 'Mrs Nab, it might become you to be more civil;
If your money be gone, as a learned *Divine* sayd, d'ye see,
You are no text for my handling; so take that from me:
I was never taken for a *Conjurer* before, I'd have you to know.'
'Lord,' said I, 'don't be angry, I am sure I never thought you so;
You know I honour the cloth; I design to be a Parson's wife, –
I never took one in *your coat* for a conjurer in all my life.'
With that he twisted his girdle at me like a rope, as who should say,
'Now you may go hang yourself for me!' and so went away.
Well: I thought I should have swoon'd. 'Lord!' said I, 'what shall
          I do?
I have lost my money, and shall lose my true love too!'
Then my lord call'd me: 'Harry,' said my lord, 'don't cry;
I'll give you something toward thy loss:' 'And,' says my lady, 'so
          will I.'
'Oh! but,' said I, 'what if, after all, the Chaplain won't come to?'
For that, he said (an't please your Excellencies) I must petition you.
The premises tenderly consider'd, I desire your Excellencies'
          protection,
And that I may have a share in next Sunday's collection;
And, over and above, that I may have your Excellencies' letter,
With an order for the Chaplain aforesaid or, instead of him, a
          better:
And then your poor petitioner, both night and day,
Or the Chaplain (for 'tis his trade,) as in duty bound, shall ever
          pray.'

JONATHAN SWIFT

Satire upon the Heads;
or, Never a Barrel the Better Herring

O Cambridge, attend
To the Satire I've pen'd
On the Heads of thy Houses,
Thou Seat of the Muses!

Know the Master of Jesus
Does hugely displease us;
The Master of Maudlin
In the same dirt is dawdling;
The Master of Sidney
Is of the same kidney;
The Master of Trinity
To him bears affinity;
As the Master of Keys
Is as like as two pease,
So the Master of Queens'
Is as like as two beans;
The Master of King's
Copies them in all things;
The Master of Catherine
Takes them all for his pattern;
The Master of Clare
Hits them all to a hair;
The Master of Christ
By the rest is enticed;
But the Master of Emmanuel
Follows them like a spaniel;
The Master of Benet
Is of the like tenet;
The Master of Pembroke
Has from them his system took;

The Master of Peter's
Has all the same features;
The Master of St John's
Like the rest of the Dons.

P.S. – As to Trinity Hall
We say nothing at all.

THOMAS GRAY

An Expostulation

When late I attempted your pity to move,
  Why seem'd you so deaf to my pray'rs?
Perhaps it was right to dissemble your love –
  But – Why did you kick me downstairs?

ISAAC BICKERSTAFF

(also attributed to J. P. KEMBLE)

On a certain Methodist-teacher being caught in Bed with his Maid

'You a Magistrate chief,' his wife tauntingly said,
'You a Methodist-Teacher! and caught with your Maid!
'A delicate Text this you've chosen to *handle*
'And fine *holding forth*, without Daylight or Candle!'
Quoth Gabriel, 'My Dear, as I hope for Salvation,
'You make in your Anger a wrong Application;
'This evening I taught *how frail our Condition;*
'And the good Maid and I were but at – Repetition.'

ANON.

Rich and Poor;
or, Saint and Sinner

The poor man's sins are glaring;
In the face of ghostly warning
   He is caught in the fact
   Of an overt act —
Buying greens on Sunday morning.

The rich man's sins are hidden
In the pomp of wealth and station;
   And escape the sight
   Of the children of light,
Who are wise in their generation.

The rich man has a kitchen,
And cooks to dress his dinner;
   The poor who would roast
   To the baker's must post,
And thus becomes a sinner.

The rich man has a cellar,
And a ready butler by him;
   The poor must steer
   For his pint of beer
Where the Saint can't choose but spy him.

The rich man's painted windows
Hide the concerts of the quality;
   The poor can but share
   A crack'd fiddle in the air,
Which offends all sound morality.

The rich man is invisible
In the crowd of his gay society;
    But the poor man's delight
    Is a sore in the sight,
And a stench in the nose of piety.

T. L. PEACOCK

All Saints

In a church which is furnish'd with mullion and gable,
    With altar and reredos, with gargoyle and groin,
The penitent's dresses are sealskin and sable,
    The odour of sanctity's eau-de-Cologne.
But only could Lucifer, flying from Hades,
    Gaze down on this crowd with its panniers and paints.
He would say, as he looked at the lords and the ladies,
    'Oh, where is ALL SINNERS', if this is ALL SAINTS'?'

EDMUND YATES

On Moll Batchelor

Beneath in the Dust, the mouldy old Crust
Of *Moll Batchelor* lately was shoven,
Who was skill'd in the Arts of Pyes, Custards and Tarts,
And every Device of the Oven.
When she'd liv'd long enough, she made her last Puff,
A Puff by her Husband much prais'd;
And here she doth lie, and makes a Dirt Pye,
In Hopes that her Crust may be rais'd.

ANON.

The Song Against Grocers

God made the wicked Grocer
For a mystery and a sign,
That men might shun the awful shops
And go to inns to dine;
Where the bacon's on the rafter
And the wine is in the wood,
And God that made good laughter
Has seen that they are good.

The evil-hearted Grocer
Would call his mother 'Ma'am',
And bow at her and bob at her,
Her aged soul to damn,
And rub his horrid hands and ask
What article was next,
Though *mortis in articulo*
Should be her proper text.

His props are not his children,
But pert lads underpaid,
Who call out 'Cash!' and bang about
To work his wicked trade;
He keeps a lady in a cage
Most cruelly all day,
And makes her count and calls her 'Miss'
Until she fades away.

The righteous minds of innkeepers
Induce them now and then
To crack a bottle with a friend
Or treat unmoneyed men,
But who hath seen the Grocer
Treat housemaids to his teas

Or crack a bottle of fish-sauce
Or stand a man a cheese?

He sells us sands of Araby
As sugar for cash down;
He sweeps his shop and sells the dust
The purest salt in town,
He crams with cans of poisoned meat
Poor subjects of the King,
And when they die by thousands
Why, he laughs like anything.

The wicked Grocer groces
In spirits and in wine,
Not frankly and in fellowship
As men in inns do dine;
But packed with soap and sardines
And carried off by grooms,
For to be snatched by Duchesses
And drunk in dressing-rooms.

The hell-instructed Grocer
Has a temple made of tin,
And the ruin of good innkeepers
Is loudly urged therein;
But now the sands are running out
From sugar of a sort,
The Grocer trembles; for his time,
Just like his weight, is short.

G. K. CHESTERTON

Lines to a Don

Remote and ineffectual Don
That dared attack my Chesterton,
With that poor weapon, half-impelled,
Unlearnt, unsteady, hardly held,
Unworthy for a tilt with men –
Your quavering and corroded pen;
Don poor at Bed and worse at Table,
Don pinched, Don starved, Don miserable;
Don stuttering, Don with roving eyes,
Don nervous, Don of crudities;
Don clerical, Don ordinary,
Don self-absorbed and solitary;
Don here-and-there, Don epileptic;
Don puffed and empty, Don dyspeptic;
Don middle-class, Don sycophantic,
Don dull, Don brutish, Don pedantic;
Don hypocritical, Don bad,
Don furtive, Don three-quarters mad;
Don (since a man must make an end),
Don that shall never be my friend.

Don different from those regal Dons!
With hearts of gold and lungs of bronze,
Who shout and bang and roar and bawl
The Absolute across the hall,
Or sail in amply bellying gown
Enormous through the Sacred Town,
Bearing from College to their homes
Deep cargoes of gigantic tomes;
Dons admirable! Dons of Might!
Uprising on my inward sight
Compact of ancient tales, and port,
And sleep – and learning of a sort.

Dons English, worthy of the land;
Dons rooted; Dons that understand.
Good Dons perpetual that remain
A landmark, walling in the plain –
The horizon of my memories –
Like large and comfortable trees.

Don very much apart from these,
Thou scapegoat Don, thou Don devoted,
Don to thine own damnation quoted,
Perplexed to find thy trivial name
Reared in my verse to lasting shame.
Don dreadful, rasping Don and wearing,
Repulsive Don – Don past all bearing.
Don of the cold and doubtful breath,
Don despicable, Don of death;
Don nasty, skimpy, silent, level;
Don evil; Don that serves the devil.
Don ugly – that makes fifty lines.
There is a Canon which confines
A Rhymed Octosyllabic Curse
If written in Iambic Verse
To fifty lines. I never cut;
I far prefer to end it – but
Believe me I shall soon return.
My fires are banked, but still they burn
To write some more about the Don
That dared attack my Chesterton.

HILAIRE BELLOC

A Glass of Beer

The lanky hank of a she in the inn over there,
Nearly killed me for asking the loan of a glass of beer;
May the devil grip the whey-faced slut by the hair,
And beat bad manners out of her skin for a year.

That parboiled ape, with the toughest jaw you will see
On virtue's path, and a voice that would rasp the dead,
Came roaring and raging the minute she looked at me,
And threw me out of the house on the back of my head!

If I asked her master he'd give me a cask a day;
But she, with the beer at hand, not a gill would arrange!
May she marry a ghost and bear him a kitten, and may
The High King of Glory permit her to get the mange.

JAMES STEPHENS (*from the Irish*)

Johnny Dow

Wha lies here?
I, Johnny Dow.
Hoo! Johnny is that you?
Ay, man, but a'm dead now.

ANON.

On Miss Arabella Young

Here lies, returned to clay,
Miss Arabella Young,
Who on the first of May
Began to hold her tongue.

ANON.

The Pessimist

Nothing to do but work,
  Nothing to eat but food,
Nothing to wear but clothes,
  To keep one from going nude.

Nothing to breathe but air,
  Quick as a flash 'tis gone;
Nowhere to fall but off,
  Nowhere to stand but on.

Nothing to comb but hair,
  Nowhere to sleep but in bed,
Nothing to weep but tears,
  Nothing to bury but dead.

Nothing to sing but songs,
  Ah, well, alas! alack!
Nowhere to go but out,
  Nowhere to come but back.

Nothing to see but sights,
  Nothing to quench but thirst,
Nothing to have but what we've got.
  Thus through life we are cursed.

Nothing to strike but a gait;
  Everything moves that goes.
Nothing at all but common sense
  Can ever withstand these woes.

B. J. KING

How Beastly the Bourgeois is

How beastly the bourgeois is
especially the male of the species –

Presentable, eminently presentable
Shall I make you a present of him?

Isn't he handsome? isn't he healthy? Isn't he a fine specimen?
doesn't he look the fresh clean englishman, outside?
Isn't it god's own image? tramping his thirty miles a day
after partridges, or a little rubber ball?
wouldn't you like to be like that, well off, and quite the thing?

Oh, but wait!
Let him meet a new emotion, let him be faced with another man's
        need.
Let him come home to a bit of moral difficulty, let life face him with
        a new demand on his understanding
and then watch him go soggy, like a wet meringue.
Watch him turn into a mess, either a fool or a bully.
Just watch the display of him, confronted with a new demand on
        his intelligence,
a new life-demand.

How beastly the bourgeois is
especially the male of the species –

Nicely groomed, like a mushroom
Standing there so sleek and erect and eyeable –
and like a fungus, living on the remains of bygone life
sucking his life out of the dead leaves of greater life than his own.

And even so, he's stale, he's been there too long.
Touch him, and you'll find he's all gone inside
just like an old mushroom, all wormy inside, and hollow
under a smooth skin and an upright appearance.

Full of seething, wormy, hollow feelings
rather nasty –
How beastly the bourgeois is!

Standing in their thousands, these appearances, in damp England.
What a pity they can't all be kicked over
like sickening toadstools, and left to melt back, swiftly
into the soil of England.

D. H. LAWRENCE

The Oxford Voice

When you hear it languishing
and hooing and cooing and sidling through the front teeth,
      the oxford voice,
         or worse still
    the would-be oxford voice
you don't even laugh any more, you can't.

For every blooming bird is an Oxford cuckoo nowadays,
you can't sit on a bus or in the tube
but it breathes gently and languishingly in the back of your neck.

And oh, so seductively superior, so seductively
      self effacingly
      deprecatingly
         superior –

> We wouldn't insist on it for a moment
> but we are
> we are
> you admit we are
> superior. –

D. H. LAWRENCE

Next to of Course God

'next to of course god america i
love you land of the pilgrims and so forth oh
say can you see by the dawn's early my
country 'tis of centuries come and go
and are no more what of it we should worry
in every language even deaf and dumb
My sons acclaim your glorious name by gorry
by jingo and by gee by gosh by gum
Why talk of beauty what could be more beautiful than these heroic happy dead
Who rushed like lions to the roaring slaughter
they did not stop to think they died instead
then shall the voice of liberty be mute?'

He spoke. And drank rapidly a glass of water.

E. E. CUMMINGS

A Politician

a politician is an arse upon
which everyone has sat except a man.

E. E. CUMMINGS

England Expects

Let us pause to consider the English,

Who when they pause to consider themselves they get all reticently
      thrilled and tinglish,

Because every Englishman is convinced of one thing, viz:

That to be an Englishman is to belong to the most exclusive club
      there is:

A club to which benighted bounders of Frenchmen and Germans
      and Italians et cetera cannot even aspire to belong,

Because they don't even speak English, and the Americans are
      worst of all because they speak it wrong.

Englishmen are distinguished by their traditions and ceremonials,

And also by their affection for their colonies and their contempt for
      the colonials.

When foreigners ponder world affairs, why sometimes by doubts
      they are smitten,

But Englishmen know instinctively that what the world needs most
      is whatever is best for Great Britain.

They have a splendid navy and they conscientiously admire it,

And every English schoolboy knows that John Paul Jones was only
      an unfair American pirate.

English people disclaim sparkle and verve,

But speak without reservations of their Anglo-Saxon reserve.

After listening to little groups of English ladies and gentlemen at
      cocktail parties and in hotels and Pullmans, of defining
      Anglo-Saxon reserve I despair,

But I think it consists of assuming that nobody else is there,

And I shudder to think where Anglo-Saxon reserve ends when I
      consider where it begins,

Which in a few high-pitched statements of what one's income is
      and just what foods give one a rash and whether one and
      one's husband or wife sleep in a double bed or twins.

All good Englishmen go to Oxford or Cambridge and they all
      write and publish books before their graduation,

And I often wondered how they did it until I realized that they have
　　　to do it because their genteel accents are so developed that
　　　they can no longer understand each other's spoken words
　　　so the written word is their only means of inter-
　　　communication.

England is the last home of the aristocracy, and the art of protecting
　　　the aristocracy from the encroachments of commerce has
　　　been raised to quite an art.

Because in America a rich butter-and-egg man is only a rich butter-
　　　and-egg man or at most an honorary LLD of some hungry
　　　university, but in England he is Sir Benjamin Buttery, Bart.

Anyhow, I think the English people are sweet,

And we might as well get used to them because when they slip and
　　　fall they always land on their own or somebody else's feet.

OGDEN NASH

Two Footnotes

I

Once for candy cook had stolen
X was punished by Papa;
When he asked where babies came from
He was lied to by Mamma.

Now the city streets are waiting
To mislead him, and he must
Keep an eye on aged beggars
Lest they strike him in disgust.

2

When statesmen gravely say – 'We must be realistic –'
The chances are they're weak and therefore pacifistic:
But when they speak of Principles – look out – perhaps
Their generals are already poring over maps.

W. H. AUDEN

WHIMS AND ODDITIES

A New Song of New Similies

My passion is as mustard strong;
 I sit all sober sad;
Drunk as a piper all day long,
 Or like a March-hare mad.

Round as a hoop the bumpers flow;
 I drink, yet can't forget her;
For, though as drunk as David's sow,
 I love her still the better.

Pert as a pear-monger I'd be,
 If Molly were but kind;
Cool as a cucumber could see
 The rest of womankind.

Like a stuck pig I gaping stare,
 And eye her o'er and o'er;
Lean as a rake with sighs and care,
 Sleek as a mouse before.

Plump as a partridge was I known,
 And soft as silk my skin,
My cheeks as fat as butter grown;
 But as a groat now thin!

I, melancholy as a cat,
 And kept awake to weep;
But she, insensible of that,
 Sound as a top can sleep.

Hard is her heart as flint or stone,
 She laughs to see me pale;

And merry as a grig is grown,
    And brisk as bottled ale.

The God of Love at her approach
    Is busy as a bee;
Hearts, sound as any bell or roach,
    Are smit and sigh like me.

Ay me! as thick as hops or hail,
    The fine men crowd about her;
But soon as dead as a door nail
    Shall I be, if without her.

Straight as my leg her shape appears;
    O were we join'd together!
My heart would be scot-free from cares,
    And lighter than a feather.

As fine as fivepence is her mien,
    No drum was ever tighter;
Her glance is as the razor keen,
    And not the sun is brighter.

As soft as pap her kisses are,
    Methinks I taste them yet;
Brown as a berry is her hair,
    Her eyes as black as jet:

As smooth as glass, as white as curds,
    Her pretty hand invites;
Sharp as a needle are her words;
    Her wit, like pepper, bites:

Brisk as a body-louse she trips,
    Clean as a penny drest;

Sweet as a rose her breath and lips,
    Round as the globe her breast.

Full as an egg was I with glee;
    And happy as a king.
Good Lord! how all men envy'd me!
    She lov'd like any thing.

But false as hell! she, like the wind,
    Chang'd, as her sex must do;
Though seeming as the turtle kind,
    And like the gospel true.

If I and Molly could agree,
    Let who would take Peru!
Great as an emperor should I be,
    And richer than a Jew.

Till you grow tender as a chick,
    I'm dull as any post;
Let us, like burs, together stick,
    And warm as any toast.

You'll know me truer than a dye;
    And wish me better speed;
Flat as a flounder when I lie,
    And as a herring dead.

Sure as a gun, she'll drop a tear,
    And sigh, perhaps, and wish,
When I am rotten as a pear,
    And mute as any fish.

JOHN GAY

The Campaign 1768

Fiat Justitia, Ruat Coelum,
We'll maul the rogues if we can fell 'em.
Justitia Fiat, Coelum Ruat,
Be sure the gun you level true at
Coelum, Justitia, Ruat, Fiat,
And shoot the man I cock my eye at.
Justitia, Fiat, Ruat, Coelum,
Obey the words of Justice Gillam,
And if the rascals halloo – kill 'em.

CAPT. T.

To a Friend

Thou swear'st thou'lt drink no more: kind heav'n, send
Me such a cook or coachman, but no friend.

ANON.

To an Acquaintance

Thou speakest always ill of me,
I always speak well of thee:
But, spite of all our noise and pother,
The world believes nor one, nor t'other.

ANON.

On Cloe

Bright as the day, and as the morning fair,
Such Cloe is – and common as the air.

GEORGE GRANVILLE, LORD LANSDOWNE

Mrs Mary Blaize

Good people all, with one accord,
    Lament for Madam Blaize,
Who never wanted a good word –
    From those who spoke her praise.

The needy seldom pass'd her door,
    And always found her kind;
She freely lent to all the poor –
    Who left a pledge behind.

She strove the neighbourhood to please
    With manners wondrous winning;
And never followed wicked ways –
    Unless when she was sinning.

At church, in silks and satins new
    With hoop of monstrous size,
She never slumbered in her pew –
    But when she shut her eyes.

Her love was sought, I do aver,
    By twenty beaux and more;
The King himself has followed her –
    When she has walk'd before.

But now, her wealth and finery fled,
    Her hangers-on cut short-all:
The doctors found, when she was dead, –
    Her last disorder mortal.

Let us lament, in sorrow sore,
    For Kent Street well may say,

That had she lived a twelvemonth more, –
   She had not died to-day.

                    OLIVER GOLDSMITH

Elegy on the Death of a Mad Dog

Good people all, of every sort,
   Give ear unto my song;
And if you find it wond'rous short,
   It cannot hold you long.

In Islington there was a man,
   Of whom the world might say,
That still a godly race he ran,
   Whene'er he went to pray.

A kind and gentle heart he had,
   To comfort friends and foes;
The naked every day he clad,
   When he put on his clothes.

And in that town a dog was found,
   As many dogs there be,
Both mongrel, puppy, whelp, and hound,
   And curs of low degree.

This dog and man at first were friends;
   But when a pique began,
The dog, to gain some private ends,
   Went mad and bit the man.

Around from all the neighbouring streets
   The wond'ring neighbours ran,

And swore the dog had lost its wits,
  To bite so good a man.

The wound it seem'd both sore and sad
  To every Christian eye;
And while they swore the dog was mad,
  They swore the man would die.

But soon a wonder came to light,
  That showed the rogues they lied:
The man recover'd of the bite,
  The dog it was that died.

OLIVER GOLDSMITH

Extempore

ON THE DEATH OF EDWARD PURDON

Here lies poor Ned Purdon, from misery freed,
  Who long was a bookseller's hack;
He led such a damnable life in this world,
  I don't think he'll ever come back.

OLIVER GOLDSMITH

To a Living Author

Your comedy I've read, my friend,
  And like the half you pilfered best;
Be sure the piece you yet may mend –
  Take courage, man, and steal the rest.

ANON.

The March to Moscow

The Emperor Nap he would set off
On a summer excursion to Moscow;
The fields were green and the sky was blue,
Morbleu! Parbleu!
What a splendid excursion to Moscow!

The Emperor Nap he talk'd so big
That he frighten'd Mr Roscoe.
And Counsellor Brougham was all in a fume
At the thought of the march to Moscow:
The Russians, he said, they were undone,
And the great Fee-Faw-Fum
Would presently come.
With a hop, step, and jump, unto London,
For, as for his conquering Russia,
However some persons might scoff it,
Do it he could, do it he would,
And from doing it nothing would come but good,
And nothing would call him off it.

But the Russians stoutly they turned to
Upon the road to Moscow.
Nap had to fight his way all through;
They could fight, though they could not parlez-vous;
But the fields were green, and the sky was blue,
Morbleu! Parbleu!
But to march back again from Moscow.

The Russians they stuck close to him
All on the road from Moscow —
And Shouvaloff he shovell'd them off,
And Markoff he mark'd them off,
And Krosnoff he cross'd them off,

And Touchkoff he touch'd them off,
And Boroskoff he bored them off,
And Kutousoff he cut them off,
And Parenzoff he pared them off,
And Worronzoff he worried them off,
And Doctoroff he doctor'd them off,
And Rodinoff he flogg'd them off.
And, last of all, an Admiral came,
A terrible man with a terrible name,
A name which you all know by sight very well,
But which no one can speak, and no one can spell.

And then came on the frost and snow
    All on the road from Moscow.
Worse and worse every day the elements grew,
The fields were so white and the sky was so blue,
        Sacrebleu! Ventrebleu!
  What a horrible journey from Moscow.

Too cold upon the road was he;
Too hot he had been at Moscow;
But colder and hotter he may be,
  For the grave is colder than Muscovy;
And a place there is to be kept in view,
Where the fire is red, and the brimstone blue,
        Morbleu! Parbleu!
But there he must stay for a very long day,
For from thence there is no stealing away,
  As there was on the road from Moscow.

                                    (*abridged*)

                            ROBERT SOUTHEY

Faithless Nellie Gray

Ben Battle was a soldier bold,
  And used to war's alarms;
But a cannon-ball took off his legs,
  So he laid down his arms.

Now as they bore him off the field,
  Said he, 'Let others shoot,
For here I leave my second leg,
  And the Forty-second Foot!'

The army-surgeons made him limbs:
  Said he: – 'They're only pegs:
But there's as wooden members quite
  As represent my legs!'

Now Ben he loved a pretty maid,
  Her name was Nellie Gray:
So he went to pay her his devours
  When he'd devoured his pay!

But when he called on Nellie Gray,
  She made him quite a scoff;
And when she saw his wooden legs
  Began to take them off!

'O, Nellie Gray! O, Nellie Gray!
  Is this your love so warm?
The love that loves a scarlet coat
  Should be more uniform!'

She said, 'I loved a soldier once,
  For he was blythe and brave;

But I will never have a man
 With both legs in the grave!

'Before you had those timber toes,
 Your love I did allow,
But then, you know, you stand upon
 Another footing now!'

'O, Nellie Gray! O, Nellie Gray!
 For all your jeering speeches,
At duty's call, I left my legs
 In Badajos's *breaches*!'

'Why, then,' she said, 'you've lost the feet
 Of legs in war's alarms,
And now you cannot wear your shoes
 Upon your feats of arms!'

'Oh, false and fickle Nellie Gray;
 I know why you refuse: —
Though I've no feet — some other man
 Is standing in my shoes!

'I wish I ne'er had seen your face;
 But now, a long farewell!
For you will be my death, alas!
 You will not be my Nell!'

Now when he went from Nellie Gray,
 His heart so heavy got —
And life was such a burthen grown,
 It made him take a knot!

So round his melancholy neck,
 A rope he did entwine,

And, for his second time in life,
   Enlisted in the Line!

One end he tied around a beam,
   And then removed his pegs,
And as his legs were off, – of course
   He soon was off his legs!

And there he hung, till he was dead
   As any nail in town, –
For though distress had cut him up,
   It could not cut him down!

A dozen men sat on his corpse,
   To find out why he died –
And they buried Ben in four cross-roads,
   With a *stake* in his inside!

                              THOMAS HOOD

Mary's Ghost

A PATHETIC BALLAD

'Twas in the middle of the night,
   To sleep young William tried;
When Mary's ghost came stealing in,
   And stood at his bed-side.

O William dear! O William dear!
   My rest eternal ceases;
Alas! my everlasting peace
   Is broken into pieces.

I thought the last of all my cares
   Would end with my last minute;

But tho' I went to my long home,
   I didn't stay long in it.

The body-snatchers they have come,
   And made a snatch at me;
It's very hard them kind of men
   Won't let a body be!

You thought that I was buried deep,
   Quite decent like and chary,
But from her grave in Mary-bone,
   They've come and boned your Mary.

The arm that used to take your arm
   Is took to Dr Vyse;
And both my legs are gone to walk
   The hospital at Guy's.

I vowed that you should have my hand,
   But fate gives us denial;
You'll find it there, at Dr Bell's,
   In spirits and a phial.

As for my feet, the little feet
   You used to call so pretty,
There's one, I know, in Bedford Row,
   The t'other's in the City.

I can't tell where my head is gone,
   But Doctor Carpue can;
As for my trunk, it's all packed up
   To go by Pickford's van.

I wish you'd go to Mr P.
   And save me such a ride;

I don't half like the outside place,
  They've took for my inside.

The cock it crows – I must be gone!
  My William, we must part!
But I'll be yours in death, altho'
  Sir Astley has my heart.

Don't go to weep upon my grave,
  And think that there I be;
They haven't left an atom there
  Of my anatomie.

                    THOMAS HOOD

Epitaph

ON A DOCTOR OF DIVINITY

Here lies a Doctor of Divinity
  He was a fellow of Trinity;
He knew as much about Divinity
  As other fellows do of Trinity.

                    RICHARD PORSON

On the Learning of the Germans

The Germans in Greek
Are sadly to seek;
Not five in five score,
But ninety-five more:
All save one HERMAN,
And HERMAN's a German.

                    RICHARD PORSON

Under-Currents

The poet who regards his youth
Through the horn spectacles of truth,
And lives to crave for what he knows,
Decays before the dying rose.
I find fruition in the churn
Which other people merely turn;
I gather at a public-house,
A theatre or a drive for grouse,
The sympathies which shed their coats
And walk about in buttoned boots
Before the stereoscopic sigh
Of histrions who atrophy
The dear complexities of home
And cower when the curry-comb
Of Pragmatist or Determinist
Explores a rib or strains a wrist.
He may, if so he chooses to,
Beneath the unction of the lawn
Unveil the feelers of the prawn,
Or from the lobster-pots of sin
Extract a pensive Paladin.
It all depends upon the view;
One man may black, another blue,
A fortune or a tennis-shoe.
And every ivy-leaf is meant
To be a little different
From every other ivy-leaf.
These are the primal and the chief
Desiderata he must have,
If he, the poet, would engrave
With a blue pencil, not a slate,
The deeds and acts and future state

Of Beauty in the dinner-dress
Of undiscovered Artlessness.

SANDYS WASON

Town

I met a clergymanly man,
    Prostrated in the Strand,
He sucked a brace of oranges;
    One orange in each hand.

He had a gentle racial air,
    He wore the clothes one wears;
The parting of his ample hair
    Had been there thirty years.

He held his cheek up to the sun;
    He let the sunlight fall
Half in contempt and half in fun
    But bitterly withal.

His words were few and special words;
    They calmed the throbs that rose
Like crumbs one offers to the birds
    Or biscuits to the does.

Before he spoke, I realized
    How false conventions are;
I sized him up like one who sized
    A cocktail at a bar.

He spoke in minuet of sound.
    I listened all the while

'Life's Little Ironies' went round
   The Gentlewomen's Mile.

It was not that his words were rare
   Or few and far between.
They had the crisp conclusive air
   Of some stray pleiocene,

Or some vague far-off dim trombone,
   Held lengthwise to the breast,
The rapt reverberate monotone
   Of working-men at rest.

He said: 'I round in scarlet kilts
   The Mulberry-bush of Life;
And carve the nightingales of Hope
   With Memory's carving-knife.

'I keep my matches in a box,
   I strike them on the lid,
I climb above the tidal rocks
   Ahasuerus did.

'I take away the strain of life,
   I walk away its throes;
O, I keep couched within my heart
   The Romaunt of the Rose!

'I am a man as men are made;
   I have the feelings men
Deny or gratify in trade
   Or chaffer with a pen.

'I kept a shop in Araby,
   The world was clean and young;

My typist was a Caribee,
   Obese but over-strung.

'I paid him for the work he did
   By piece-time or the hour.
The doorway of the shop was hid
   With pomegranates in flower.

'My customers were Turkish nuns,
   The novices, Chocktaws;
They lived on septic Sally Lunns,
   Devoted to the cause.'

And still at every Christmas time
   I see the old man sit
And suck on at his oranges
   And sit and sit and sit.

SANDYS WASON

The Young Person of Mullion

There was a young person of Mullion,
Intent upon marrying bullion;
   By some horrible fluke,
   She jilted a duke
And had to elope with a scullion.

SANDYS WASON

The Old Priest of Benares

There was an old priest of Benares
Who kept twenty-three hybrid canaries.
   But the noise the birds made
   When the gentleman prayed
Eclipsed all their other vagaries.

SANDYS WASON

Poetical Economy

What hours I spent of precious time,
  What pints of ink I used to waste,
Attempting to secure a rhyme
  To suit the public taste,
Until I found a simple plan
Which makes the lamest lyric scan!

When I've a syllable de trop,
  I cut it off, without apol.:
This verbal sacrifice, I know,
  May irritate the schol.;
But all must praise my dev'lish cunn.
Who realize that Time is Mon.

My sense remains as clear as cryst.,
  My style as pure as any Duch.
Who does not boast a bar sinist.
  Upon her fam. escutch.;
And I can treat with scornful pit.
The sneers of ev'ry captious crit.

I gladly publish to the pop.
  A scheme of which I make no myst.,
And beg my fellow scribes to cop.
  This-labour-saving syst.
I offer it to the consid.
Of ev'ry thoughtful individ.

The author, working like a beav.,
  His readers' pleasure could redoub.
Did he but now and then abbrev.
  The work he gives his pub.

(This view I most partic. suggest
To A. C. Bens. and G. K. Chest.)

If Mr Caine rewrote The Scape.,
    And Miss Correll condensed Barabb.,
What could they save in foolscap pape.
    Did they but cult. the hab.,
Which teaches people to suppress
All syllables that are unnec.!

If playwrights would but thus dimin.
    The length of time each drama takes,
(The Second Mrs Tanq. by Pin.
    Or even Ham., by Shakes.)
We could maintain a watchful att.
When at a Mat. on Wed. or Sat.

Have done, ye bards, with dull monot.!
    Foll. my examp., O, Stephen Phill.,
O, Owen Seam., O, William Wat.,
    O, Ella Wheeler Wil.,
And share with me the grave respons.
Of writing this amazing nons.!

                                    HARRY GRAHAM

Baby

Baby roused its father's ire
    By a cold and formal lisp.
So he placed it on the fire
    And reduced it to a crisp.
Mother said, 'Oh, stop a bit!
This is overdoing it!'

                                    HARRY GRAHAM

Nobody Loses All the Time

nobody loses all the time

i had an uncle named
Sol who was a born failure and
nearly everybody said he should have gone
into vaudeville perhaps because my Uncle Sol could
sing McCann He was A Diver on Xmas Eve like Hell Itself which
may or may not account for the fact that my Uncle

Sol indulged in that possibly most inexcusable
of all to use a highfalootin phrase
luxuries that is or to
wit farming and be
it needlessly
added

my Uncle Sol's farm
failed because the chickens
ate the vegetables so
my Uncle Sol had a
chicken farm till the
skunks ate the chickens when

my Uncle Sol
had a skunk farm but
the skunks caught cold and
died and so
my Uncle Sol imitated the
skunks in a subtle manner

or by drowning himself in the watertank
but somebody who'd given my Uncle Sol a Victor
Victrola and records while he lived presented to

him upon the auspicious occasion of his decease a
scrumptious not to mention splendiferous funeral with
tall boys in black gloves and flowers and everything and

i remember we all cried like the Missouri
when my Uncle Sol's coffin lurched because
somebody pressed a button
(and down went
my Uncle
Sol

and started a worm farm)

E. E. CUMMINGS

A Glimpse into the Great Beyond

Sir Arthur Conan Doyle is reported to have held several
conversations, since his decease, with Mr Hannen Swaffer.

Now that Sir Arthur has the run
of all the pleasures Space can offer,
might we conclude they're not much fun
since he comes back to talk to Swaffer?

EDGELL RICKWORD

Requiem

There was a young belle of old Natchez
Whose garments were always in patchez.
When comment arose
On the state of her clothes,
She drawled, 'When Ah itchez, Ah scratchez.'

OGDEN NASH

The Anatomy of Humour

'What is funny?' you ask, my child,
    Crinkling your bright-blue eye.
'Ah, that is a curious question indeed,'
    Musing, I make reply.

'Contusions are funny, not open wounds,
    And automobiles that go
Crash into trees by the highwayside;
    Industrial accidents, no.

'The habit of drink is a hundred per cent,
    But drug addiction is nil.
A nervous breakdown will get no laughs;
    Insanity surely will.

'Humour, aloof from the cigarette,
    Inhabits the droll cigar;
The middle-aged are not very funny;
    The young and the old, they are.

'So the funniest thing in the world should be
    A grandsire, drunk, insane.
Maimed in a motor accident,
    And enduring moderate pain.

'But why do you scream and yell, my child?
    Here comes your mother, my honey,
To comfort you and to lecture me
    For trying, she'll say, to be funny.'

MORRIS BISHOP

We Have Been Here Before

I think I remember this moorland,
    The tower on the tip of the tor;
I feel in the distance another existence;
    I think I have been here before.

And I think you were sitting beside me
    In a fold in the face of the fell;
For Time at its work'll go round in a circle,
    And what is befalling, befell.

'I have been here before!' I asserted,
    In a nook on a neck of the Nile.
I once in a crisis was punished by Isis,
    And you smiled, I remember your smile.

I had the same sense of persistence
    On the site of the seat of the Sioux;
I heard in the tepee the sound of a sleepy
    Pleistocene grunt. It was you.

The past made a promise, before it
    Began to begin to begone.
This limited gamut brings you again. . . . Damn it,
    How long has this got to go on?

MORRIS BISHOP

Note on Intellectuals

To the man-in-the-street, who, I'm sorry to say
    Is a keen observer of life,
The word Intellectual suggests straight away
    A man who's untrue to his wife.

W. H. AUDEN

Mythology

All my favourite characters have been
Out of all pattern and proportion;
Some living in villas by railways,
Some like Katsimbalis heard but seldom seen,
And others in banks whose sunless hands
Moved like great rats on ledgers . . .

Tibble, Gondril, Purvis, the Duke of Puke,
Shatterblossom and Dude Bowdler
Who swelled up in Jaffa and became a tree,
Hollis who had seven wives killed under him like horses
And that man of destiny.

Ramon de something who gave lectures
From an elephant; founded a society
To protect the inanimate against cruelty.
He gave asylum to aged chairs in his home,
Lampposts and crockery, everything that
Seemed to him suffering he took in
Without mockery.

The poetry was in the pity. No judgement
Disturbs people like these in their frames
O men of the Marmion class, sons of the free.

LAWRENCE DURRELL

Reflexions on Ice-Breaking

Candy
is dandy
But liquor
is quicker.

OGDEN NASH

Arizona Nature Myth

Up in the heavenly saloon
Sheriff sun and rustler moon
Gamble, stuck in the sheriff's mouth
The fag end of an afternoon.

There in the bad town of the sky
Sheriff, nervy, wonders why
He's let himself wander so far West
On his own; he looks with a smoky eye

At the rustler opposite turning white,
Lays down a king for Law, sits tight
Bluffing. On it that crooked moon
Plays an ace and shoots for the light.

Spurs, badge, and uniform red,
(It looks like blood, but he's shamming dead),
Down drops the marshal, and under cover
Crawls out dogwise, ducking his head.

But Law that don't get its man ain't Law.
Next day, faster on the draw,
Sheriff creeping up from the other side,
Blazes his way in through the back door.

But moon's not there. He's ridden out on
A galloping phenomenon,
A wonder horse, quick as light.
Moon's left town. Moon's clean gone.

JAMES MICHIE

RIGMAROLES AND
NONSENSE

The bittern with his bumpė,
The crane with his trumpė,
The swan of Maeander,
The goose and the gander,
The duck and the drake,
Shall watch at his wake;
The peacock so proud,
Because his voice is loud,
And hath a glorious tail,
He shall sing the Grail [1];
The owl, that is so foul,
Must help us to howl;
The heron so gaunt,
And the cormorant,
With the pheasant
And the gaggling gant [2],
And the churlish chough;
The knot and the ruff;
The barnacle [3], the buzzard,
With the wild mallard;
The divendop to sleep;
The waterhen to weep;
The puffin and the teal
Money they shall deal
To poorė folk at large,
That shall be their charge;
The seamew and the titmouse;
The woodcock with the long nose;
The throstling with her warbling;
The starling with her brabling;
The rook, with the osprey
That putteth fishes to a fray;

1. the Graduale.   2. gannet   3. the barnacle goose.

And the dainty curlew,
With the turtle most true.

At this *Placebo*
We may not well forgo
The countering of the coe [1];
The stork also,
That maketh his nest;
Within those walls
No broken galls
May there abide
Of cuckoldry side,
Or else philosophy
Maketh a great lie
The ostrich, that will eat
An horseshoe so great,
In the stead of meat,
Such fervent heat
His stomach doth freat;
He cannot well fly,
Nor sing tunably
Yet at a brayd [2]
He hath well assayed
To sol-fa above ela
Fa, lorell, fa, fa!
Ne quando
Male cantando [3]
The best that we can,
To make him our bell-man,
And let him ring the bells.
He can do nothing else.

JOHN SKELTON

1. Jackdaw.   2. at a push.   3. Lest ever by singing badly.

Three Jovial Huntsmen

There were three jovial huntsmen,
    As I have heard them say,
And they would go a-hunting
    All on a summer's day.

All the day they hunted,
    And nothing could they find
But a ship a-sailing,
    A-sailing with the wind.

One said it was a ship,
    The other said Nay;
The third said it was a house
    With the chimney blown away.

And all the night they hunted,
    And nothing could they find;
But the moon a-gliding,
    A-gliding with the wind.

One said it was the moon,
    The other said Nay;
The third said it was a cheese,
    And half o't cut away.

ANON.

On John Grubb

When from the chrysalis of the tomb,
I rise in rainbow-coloured plume,
My weeping friends, ye scarce will know
That I was but a Grubb below.

ANON.

If All the World were Paper

If all the world were paper,
And all the sea were inke;
And all the trees were bread and cheese,
What should we do for drinke?

If all the world were sand 'o,
Oh, then what should we lack 'o;
If as they say there were no clay,
How should we make tobacco?

If all our vessels ran 'a,
If none but had a crack 'a;
If Spanish apes eat all the grapes,
What should we do for sack 'a?

If fryers had no bald pates,
Nor nuns had no dark cloysters,
If all the seas were beans and pease,
What should we do for oysters?

If there had been no projects,
Nor none that did great wrongs;
If fidlers shall turne players all,
What should we doe for songs?

If all things were eternall,
And nothing their end bringing;
If this should be, then, how should we
Here make an end of singing?

ANON.

Epilogus Incerti Authoris

Like to the mowing tone of unspoke speeches,
Or like two lobsters clad in logick breeches;
Or like the gray fleece of a crimson catt,
Or like the moone-calfe in a slippshod hatt;
Or like the shaddow when the sunne is gone,
Or like a thought, that nev'r was thought upon:
    Even such is man who never was begotten
    Untill his children were both dead and rotten.

Like to the fiery touch-hole of a cabbage,
Or like a crablowse with his bag and baggage;
Or like the guilt reflection of the winde,
Or like the abortive issue borne behind;
Or like the four square circle of a ring,
Or like high downe a ding a ding a ding;
    Even such is man who breathlesse without a doubt
    Spake to small purpose when his tongue was out.

Like the fresh colours of a withered rose,
Or like a running verse that's writ in prose;
Or like the umbles of a tynder box,
Or like a sound man, troubled with the pox;
Or like to hobbnayles coyn'd in single pence,
Lest they should lose their preterperfect tence,
    Even such is man who dyed, and yet did laugh,
    To read these strong lines for his Epitaph.

RICHARD CORBET

On Tadlow

When Tadlow walks the streets, the paviours cry,
'God bless you, sir!' and lay their rammers by.

ABEL EDWARDS

Warning to Parents

Three children sliding on the ice
    Upon a summer's day,
It so fell out they all fell in.
    The rest they ran away.

Now had these children been at home,
    Or sliding on dry ground,
Ten thousand pounds to one penny
    They had not all been drown'd.

You parents all that children have,
    And you that eke have none,
If you would have them safe abroad,
    Pray keep them safe at home.

Sung to the tune of 'Chevy Chase'

ANON.

From
The Westminster Drollery, 1671

I saw a peacock with a fiery tail
I saw a blazing comet drop down hail
I saw a cloud wrapped with ivory wand
I saw an oak creep upon the ground
I saw a pismire swallow up a whale
I saw the sea brimful of ale
I saw a Venice glass full fifteen feet deep
I saw a well full of men's tears that weep
I saw red eyes all of a flaming fire
I saw a house bigger than the moon and higher
I saw the sun at twelve o'clock at night
I saw the man that saw this wondrous sight.

ANON.

Receipt for Stewing Veal

Take a knuckle of Veal,
You may buy it, or steal,
In a few pieces cut it,
In a Stewing pan put it,
Salt, pepper and mace
Must season this knuckle,
Then what's join'd to a place [1],
With other Herbs muckle;
That which Killed King Will [2],
And what never stands still [3],
Some sprigs of that bed [4]
Where Children are bred,
Which much you will mend, if
Both Spinnage and Endive,
And Lettuce and Beet,
With Marygold meet:
Put no water at all;
For it maketh things small:
Which, lest it should happen,
A close cover clap on;
Put this pot of Wood's mettle [5]
In a hot boiling kettle,
And there let it be,
(Mark the doctrine I teach)
About – let me see, –
Thrice as long as you preach [6].

1. Vulg. Salary.
2. Suppos'd Sorrell.
3. This is by Dr Bentley thought to be Time or Thyme.
4. Parsley. *Vide* Chamberlaine.
5. Of this composition see the Works of the Copper farthing Dean.
6. Which we suppose to be near four hours.

So skimming the fat off,
Say Grace, with your hat off
O then, with what rapture
Will it fill Dean and Chapter.

Attributed to ALEXANDER POPE

Three Young Rats

Three young rats with black felt hats,
Three young ducks with white straw flats,
Three young dogs with curling tails,
Three young cats with demi-veils,
Went out to walk with two young pigs
In satin vests and sorrel wigs;
But suddenly it chanced to rain,
And so they all went home again.

ANON.

On Certain Ladies

When other fair ones to the shades go down
Still Chloe, Flavia, Delia, stay in town:
Those ghosts of beauty wandering here reside,
And haunt the places where their honour died.

ALEXANDER POPE

Epigram

engraved on the collar of a dog which I gave to his Royal Highness
Frederick Prince of Wales

I am his Highness' dog at Kew
Pray tell me, sir, whose dog are you?

ALEXANDER POPE

The Great Panjandrum

So she went into the garden
to cut a cabbage-leaf
to make an apple-pie;
and at the same time
a great she-bear, coming down the street,
pops its head into the shop.
What! no soap?
                    So he died,
and she very imprudently married the Barber:
and there were present
the Picninnies,
            and the Joblillies,
                    and the Garyulies,
and the great Panjandrum himself,
with the little round button at top;
and they all fell to playing the game of catch-as-catch-can,
till the gunpowder ran out at the heels of their boots.

SAMUEL FOOTE

Rhyme for a Simpleton

I said, 'This horse, sir, will you shoe?'
    And soon the horse was shod.
I said, 'This deed, sir, will you do?'
    And soon the deed was dod!

I said, 'This stick, sir, will you break?
    At once the stick he broke.
I said, 'This coat, sir, will you make?'
    And soon the coat he moke!

ANON.

The House that Jack Built

And this reft house is that the which he built,
Lamented Jack! and here his malt he piled.
Cautious in vain! these rats that squeak so wild,
Squeak not unconscious of their father's guilt.
Did he not see her gleaming through the glade!
Belike 'twas she, the maiden all forlorn.
What though she milked no cow with crumpled horn,
Yet, aye she haunts the dale where erst she strayed:
And aye before her stalks her amorous knight!
Still on his thighs their wonted brogues are worn,
And through those brogues, still tattered and betorn,
His hindward charms gleam an unearthly white.

SAMUEL TAYLOR COLERIDGE

A Man of Words

A man of words and not of deeds,
Is like a garden full of weeds;
And when the weeds begin to grow,
It's like a garden full of snow;
And when the snow begins to fall,
It's like a bird upon the wall;
And when the bird away does fly,
It's like an eagle in the sky;
And when the sky begins to roar,
It's like a lion at the door;
And when the door begins to crack,
It's like a stick across your back;
And when your back begins to smart,
It's like a penknife in your heart;
And when your heart begins to bleed,
You're dead, and dead, and dead indeed.

ANON.

Nonsense Verses

Lazy-bones, lazy-bones, wake up and peep!
The cat's in the cupboard, your mother's asleep.
There you sit snoring, forgetting her ills;
Who is to give her her Bolus and Pills?
Twenty fine Angels must come into town,
All for to help you to make your new gown:
Dainty aerial Spinsters and Singers;
Aren't you ashamed to employ such white fingers?
Delicate hands, unaccustom'd to reels,
To set 'em working a poor body's wheels?
Why they came down is to me all a riddle,
And left Hallelujah broke off in the middle;
Jove's court, and the Presence angelical, cut –
To eke out the work of a lazy young slut.
Angel-duck, Angel-duck, winged and silly,
Pouring a watering-pot over a lily,
Gardener gratuitous, careless of pelf,
Leave her to water her lily herself,
Or to neglect it to death if she chuse it:
Remember the loss is her own, if she lose it.

CHARLES LAMB

In the Dumps

We're all in the dumps,
    For diamonds are trumps;
The kittens are gone to St Paul's!
    The babies are bit,
    The Moon's in a fit,
And the houses are built without walls.

ANON.

She is Far from the Land

Cables entangling her,
Shipspars for mangling her,
Ropes, sure of strangling her;
Blocks, over-dangling her;
Tiller to batter her,
Topmast to shatter her,
Tobacco to spatter her;
Boreas blustering,
Boatswain quite flustering,
Thunder-clouds mustering
To blast her with sulphur –
If the deep don't engulf her;
Sometimes fear's scrutiny
Pries out a mutiny,
Sniffs conflagration,
Or hints at starvation: –
All the sea-dangers,
Buccaneers, rangers,
Pirates and Sallee-men
Algerine galleymen,
Tornadoes and typhons,
And horrible syphons,
And submarine travels
Thro' roaring sea-navels.
Everything wrong enough,
Long-boat not long enough,
Vessel not strong enough;
Pitch marring frippery,
The deck very slippery,
And the cabin – built sloping,
The Captain a-toping,
And the mate a blasphemer,

That names his Redeemer, –
With inward uneasiness;
The cook known, by greasiness,
The victuals beslubber'd,
Her bed – in a cupboard;
Things of strange christening,
Snatched in her listening,
Blue lights and red lights
And mention of dead-lights,
And shrouds made a theme of,
Things horrid to dream of, –
And buoys in the water
To fear all exhort her;
Her friend no Leander,
Herself no sea-gander,
And ne'er a cork jacket
On board of the packet;
The breeze still a-stiffening,
The trumpet quite deafening;
Thoughts of repentance,
And doomsday and sentence;
Everything sinister,
Not a church minister, –
Pilot a blunderer,
Coral reefs under her,
Ready to sunder her;
Trunks tipsy-topsy,
The ship in a dropsy;
Waves oversurging her,
Sirens, a-dirgeing her;
Sharks all expecting her,
Swordfish dissecting her,
Crabs with their hand-vices
Punishing land vices;
Sea-dogs and unicorns,
Things with no puny horns,

Mermen carnivorous –
'Good Lord deliver us!'

THOMAS HOOD

A Nocturnal Sketch

Even is come; and from the dark Park, hark
The signal of the setting sun – one gun!
And six is sounding from the chime, prime time
To go and see the Drury-Lane Dane slain, –
Or hear Othello's jealous doubt spout out, –
Or Macbeth raving at that shade-made blade,
Denying to his frantic clutch much touch; –
Or else to see Ducrow with wide stride ride
Four horses as no other man can span;
Or in the small Olympic Pit, sit split
Laughing at Liston, while you quiz his phiz.

Anon Night comes, and with her wings brings things
Such as, with his poetic tongue, Young sung;
The gas up-blazes with its bright white light,
And paralytic watchmen prowl, howl, growl,
About the streets and take up Pall-Mall Sal,
Who, hasting to her nightly jobs, robs fobs.

Now thieves to enter for your cash, smash, crash,
Past drowsy Charley, in a deep sleep, creep,
But frightened by Policeman B.3, flee,
And while they're going, whisper low, 'No go!'
Now puss, while folks are in their beds, treads leads.
And sleepers waking, grumble – 'Drat that cat!'
Who in the gutter caterwauls, squalls, mauls
Some feline foe, and screams in shrill ill-will.

Now Bulls of Bashan, of a prize size, rise
In childish dreams, and with a roar gore poor
Georgy, or Charley, or Billy, willy-nilly; –
But Nursemaid, in a nightmare rest, chest-pressed,
Dreameth of one of her old flames, James Games,
And that she hears – what faith is man's! – Ann's banns
And his, from Reverend Mr Rice, twice, thrice:
White ribbons flourish, and a stout shout out,
That upward goes, shows Rose knows those bows' woes!

THOMAS HOOD

Sonnet found in a Deserted Mad-House

Oh that my soul a marrow-bone might seize!
For the old egg of my desire is broken,
Spilled is the pearly white and spilled the yolk, and
As the mild melancholy contents grease
My path the shorn lamb baas like bumblebees.
Time's trashy purse is as a taken token
Or like a thrilling recitation, spoken
By mournful mouths filled full of mirth and cheese.

And yet, why should I clasp the earthful urn?
Or find the frittered fig that felt the fast?
Or choose to chase the cheese around the churn?
Or swallow any pill from out the past?
Ah no, Love, not while your hot kisses burn
Like a potato riding on the blast.

ANON.

A Polka Lyric

Qui nunc dancere vult modo,
Wants to dance in the fashion, oh!
Discere debet – ought to know,
Kickere floor cum heel and toe,
   One, two, three,
   Hop with me,
Whirligig, twirligig, rapide.

Polkam jungere, Virgo, vis,
Will you join the polka, miss?
Liberius – most willingly,
Sic agimus – then let us try:
   Nunc vide,
   Skip with me,
Whirlabout, roundabout, celere.

Tum laeva cito, tum dextra,
First to the left, and then t'other way;
Aspice retro in vultu,
You look at her, and she looks at you.
   Das palmam
   Change hands, ma'am;
Celere – run away, just in sham.

BARCLAY PHILIPS

Upon St George for England

St George, to save a maid, the dragon slew;
A pretty tale, if all that's said be true;
Some say there was no dragon; and 'tis said,
There was no George; I wish there was a maid.

ANON.

Evidence Read at the Trial of the Knave of Hearts

They told me you had been to her,
    And mentioned me to him:
She gave me a good character,
    But said I could not swim.

He sent them word I had not gone,
    (We know it to be true):
If she should push the matter on,
    What would become of you?

I gave her one, they gave him two,
    You gave us three or more;
They all returned from him to you,
    Though they were mine before.

If I or she should chance to be
    Involved in this affair,
He trusts to you to set them free,
    Exactly as we were.

My notion was that you had been
    (Before she had this fit)
An obstacle that came between
    Him, and ourselves, and it.

Don't let him know she liked them best,
    For this must ever be
A secret, kept from all the rest,
    Between yourself and me.

                                LEWIS CARROLL

Humpty Dumpty's Recitation

In winter, when the fields are white,
I sing this song for your delight —

In spring, when woods are getting green,
I'll try and tell you what I mean.

In summer, when the days are long,
Perhaps you'll understand the song:

In autumn, when the leaves are brown,
Take pen and ink, and write it down.

I sent a message to the fish:
I told them 'This is what I wish.'

The little fishes of the sea
They sent an answer back to me.

The little fishes' answer was
'We cannot do it, Sir, because —'

I sent to them again to say
'It will be better to obey.'

The fishes answered with a grin
'Why, what a temper you are in!'

I told them once, I told them twice:
They would not listen to advice.

I took a kettle large and new,
Fit for the deed I had to do.

My heart went hop, my heart went thump ;
I filled the kettle at the pump.

Then some one came to me and said,
'The little fishes are in bed.'

I said to him, I said it plain,
'Then you must wake them up again.'

I said it very loud and clear ;
I went and shouted in his ear.

But he was very stiff and proud;
He said 'You needn't shout so loud!'

And he was very proud and still;
He said 'I'd go and wake them, if —'

I took a corkscrew from the shelf:
I went to wake them up myself.

And when I found the door was locked,
I pulled and pushed and kicked and knocked.

And when I found the door was shut
I tried to turn the handle, but —

LEWIS CARROLL

The Voice of the Lobster

' 'Tis the voice of the Lobster; I heard him declare,
"You have baked me too brown, I must sugar my hair."
As a duck with its eyelids, so he with his nose
Trims his belt and his buttons, and turns out his toes.

When the sands are all dry, he is gay as a lark,
And will talk in contemptuous tones of the Shark:
But, when the tide rises and sharks are around,
His voice has a timid and tremulous sound.

'I passed by his garden, and marked, with one eye,
How the Owl and the Panther were sharing a pie:
The Panther took pie-crust, and gravy, and meat,
While the Owl had the dish as its share of the treat.
When the pie was all finished, the Owl, as a boon,
Was kindly permitted to pocket the spoon:
While the Panther received knife and fork with a growl,
And concluded the banquet by – '

LEWIS CARROLL

The Mad Gardener's Song

He thought he saw an Elephant,
    That practised on a fife:
He looked again, and found it was
    A letter from his wife.
'At length I realize,' he said,
    'The bitterness of Life!'

He thought he saw a Buffalo
    Upon the chimney-piece:
He looked again, and found it was
    His Sister's Husband's Niece,
'Unless you leave this house,' he said,
    'I'll send for the Police!'

He thought he saw a Rattlesnake
    That questioned him in Greek:

He looked again, and found it was
   The Middle of Next Week.
'The one thing I regret,' he said,
   'Is that it cannot speak!'

He thought he saw a Banker's Clerk
   Descending from the 'bus:
He looked again, and found it was
   A Hippopotamus.
'If this should stay to dine,' he said,
   'There won't be much for us!'

He thought he saw a Kangaroo
   That worked a coffee-mill:
He looked again, and found it was
   A Vegetable-Pill.
'Were I to swallow this,' he said,
   'I should be very ill!'

He thought he saw a Coach-and-Four
   That stood beside his bed:
He looked again, and found it was
   A Bear without a Head.
'Poor thing,' he said, 'poor silly thing!
   It's waiting to be fed!'

He thought he saw an Albatross
   That fluttered round the lamp:
He looked again, and found it was
   A Penny-Postage-Stamp.
'You'd best be getting home,' he said,
   'The nights are very damp!'

He thought he saw a Garden-Door
   That opened with a key:

He looked again, and found it was
    A Double Rule of Three:
'And all its mystery,' he said,
    'Is clear as day to me!'

He thought he saw an Argument
    That proved he was the Pope:
He looked again, and found it was
    A Bar of Mottled Soap.
'A fact so dread,' he faintly said,
    'Extinguishes all hope!'

LEWIS CARROLL

Lines by a Humanitarian

Be lenient with lobsters, and ever kind to crabs,
And be not disrespectful to cuttle-fish or dabs;
Chase not the Cochin-China, chaff not the ox obese,
And babble not of feather-beds in company with geese.
Be tender with the tadpole, and let the limpet thrive,
Be merciful to mussels, don't skin your eels alive;
When talking to a turtle don't mention calipee –
Be always kind to animals wherever you may be.

ANON.

The Old Person of Fratton

There was an old person of Fratton
Who would go to church with his hat on.
    'If I wake up,' he said,
    'With my hat on my head,
I shall know that it hasn't been sat on.'

ANON.

Malum Opus

Prope ripam fluvii solus
A senex silently sat;
Super capitum ecce his wig,
Et wig super, ecce his hat.

Blew Zephyrus alte, acerbus,
Dum elderly gentleman sat;
Et a capite took up quite torve
Et in rivum projecit his hat.

Tunc soft maledixit the old man,
Tunc stooped from the bank where he sat
Et cum scipio poked in the water,
Conatus servare his hat.

Blew Zephyrus alte, acerbus,
The moment it saw him at that;
Et whisked his novum scratch wig,
In flumen, along with his hat.

Ab imo pectore damnavit
In coeruleus eye dolor sat;
Tunc despairingly threw in his cane
Nare cum his wig and his hat.

L'ENVOI

Contra bonos mores, don't swear,
It is wicked, you know (verbum sat),
Si this tale habet no other moral,
Mehercle! You're gratus to that!

J. A. MORGAN

A False Gallop of Analogies

There is a fine stuffed chavender,
   A chavender or chub,
That decks the rural pavender,
   The pavender or pub,
Wherein I eat my gravender,
   My gravender or grub.

How good the honest gravender!
   How snug the rustic pavender!
From sheets as sweet as lavender,
   As lavender, or lub,
I jump into my tavender,
   My tavender, or tub.

Alas! for town and clavender,
   For business and club!
They call me from my pavender
To-night; ay, there's the ravender,
   Ay, there comes in the rub!
To leave each blooming shravender,
   Each Spring-bedizened shrub,
And meet the horsey savender,
   The very forward sub,
At dinner at the clavender,
And then at billiards dravender,
   At billiards roundly drub
The self-sufficient cavender,
   The not ill-meaning cub,
Who me a bear will davender,
   A bear unfairly dub,

Because I sometimes snavender,
   Not too severely snub
His setting right the clavender,
   His teaching all the club!

Farewell to peaceful pavender,
   My river-dreaming pub,
To bed as sweet as lavender,
To homely, wholesome gravender,
And you, inspiring chavender,
   Stuff'd, chavender, or chub.

W. ST LEGER

The Old Man who said ' Hush'

There was an Old Man who said, 'Hush!
I perceive a young bird in this bush!'
   When they said, 'Is it small?'
   He replied, 'Not at all!
It is four times as big as the bush!'

EDWARD LEAR

The Old Man with a Beard

There was an Old Man with a beard,
Who sat on a horse when he reared;
   But they said, 'Never mind!
   You will fall off behind,
You propitious Old Man with a beard!'

EDWARD LEAR

I Wish I Were

I wish I were a
Elephantiaphus
And could pick off the coconuts with my nose.
But, oh! I am not,
(Alas! I cannot be)
An Elephanti –
Elephantiaphus.
But I'm a cockroach
And I'm a water-bug,
I can crawl around and hide behind the sink.

I wish I were a
Rhinoscerèeacus
And could wear an ivory toothpick in my nose.
But, oh! I am not,
(Alas! I cannot be)
A Rhinoscōri –
Rhinoscerèeacus –
But I'm a beetle
And I'm a pumpkin-bug,
I can buzz and bang my head against the wall.

I wish I were a
Hippopōpotamus
And could swim the Tigris and the broad Gangès.
But, oh! I am not,
(Alas! I cannot be)
A hippopōpo –
Hippopōpotamus –
But I'm a grasshopper
And I'm a katydid,
I can play the fiddle with my left hind-leg.

I wish I were a
Levileviathan
And had seven hundred knuckles in my spine.
But, oh! I am not,
(Alas! I cannot be)
A Levi-ikey –
A Levi-ikey-mo.
But I'm a firefly
And I'm a lightning-bug,
I can light cheroots and gaspers with my tail.

AMERICAN FOLK SONG

Motor Bus

What is this that roareth thus?
Can it be a Motor Bus?
Yes, the smell and hideous hum
Indicat Motorem Bum!
Implet in the Corn and High
Terror me Motoris Bi:
Bo Motori clamitabo
Ne Motore caedar a Bo –
Dative be or Ablative
So thou only let us live:
Whither shall thy victims flee?
Spare us, spare us, Motor Be!
Thus I sang; and still anigh
Came in hordes Motores Bi,
Et complebat omne forum
Copia Motorum Borum.
How shall wretches live like us
Cincti Bis Motoribus?
Domine, defende nos
Contra hos Motores Bos!

A. D. GODLEY

Infant Innocence

The Grizzly Bear is huge and wild
He has devoured the infant child.
The infant child is not aware
He has been eaten by the bear.

A. E. HOUSMAN

The Common Cormorant

The common cormorant or shag
Lays eggs inside a paper bag.
The reason you will see no doubt
It is to keep the lightning out.
But what these unobservant birds
Have never noticed is that herds
Of wandering bears may come with buns
And steal the bags to hold the crumbs.

ANON.

Peas

I always eat peas with honey,
I've done it all my life,
They do taste kind of funny,
But it keeps them on the knife.

ANON.

Poems

1

Captain Busby put his beard in his mouth and sucked it, then took
it out and spat on it then put it in and sucked it then walked
on down the street thinking hard.
Suddenly he put his wedding ring in his trilby hat and put the hat
on a passing kitten. Then he carefully calculated the width
of the pavement with a pair of adjustable sugar-tongs. This
done he knitted his brows. Then he walked on thinking
hard.

2

Captain Busted Busby frowned hard at a passing ceiling and fixed
his eye upon a pair of stationary taxis. Suddenly he went up
to one of them and addressed himself to the driver. He
discharged his socks and continued whistling. The taxi
saluted but he put up with it, and puckered a resigned
mouth and knitted a pair of thoughtful eyebrows.

3

M. looking out of his window with purple curtains saw Captain
Busby thoughtfully chewing a less impatient portion of his
walking-stick ostentatiously against a lamp-post. The road
was blue but Captain Busby seemed a very dark green with
ivory face (for it was night time). He frowned. He looked
up to the top of the rapidly emptying street. He cut his hair
slowly. He looked at the bottom of the street. He made
rapid measurements with a pair of adjustable sugar-tongs.
These he afterwards secreted in his trousers. He then flew
into his friend's apartment through the willingly opened
window.

4

Marcella waited for her lover outside a public house known to both
    of them. Immediately Captain Busby appeared holding a
    woman in his arms. This wasn't true thought Marcella care-
    fully, and was relieved to see that God had thrown a lamp-
    post at the Captain, temporarily disabling him.

5

He arranged himself in sugar and put himself in his bath
And prepared to breathe his last

his four bottles lay grouped around him

do your duty in this world and gather dividends from the
dog thrown at you

goodbye my children

and he died and they huskily nailed down his coffin
and put it in ten feet of soil
and grouped around him reading the will

for indeed and forever would he be
to them
just dad

6

Mother lay crying in the withdrawing room
bitterly bewailing cruel fate who with a flick of his pen
had so completely shattered the even tenour of her ways

sobbed upon the brick platform shaking her fist at every porter who
        passed
declaring cruel fate who with a flick of his pen
had so cruelly broken
the even tenour of her ways

7

she considered the porter with the cap on the side of his head fitfully
who had squandered his sweet-peas upon her
who had ridden every train and blown all whistles
to feast his evil frontal eyes on her to break the even tenour of her
        ways
she shunted her back to him
she put on her large black hat with insolent vulgarity
and deliberately smirked into his face

he was busy
he was doing his duty
he rattled the cans
he gave out composed answers to the backchat following his curt
        commands
he went on with his duty forgetting
that he had broken the even tenour of her ways

She walked thoughtfully upon a sugar-box
and would there and then have harangued the station officials to
        compel the attention of the porter

but he did not
but he could not
but he did not
and could not should as he had broken the even tenour of her ways
she thrust a carrot into his face
he gravely took it and handed it without moving a muscle of his
        face

to the dominant personality of
the station master himself

events moved indefatigably to their long-awaited climax
the station master seized the carrot and conveyed it to a drawer
        reserved for matters of importance
and seizing a document asserting his credentials and authority
motored along the platform and alighted at the lady

Madam he said coldly
your carrot is in the drawer
pray come for it or suitable measures will be taken to enforce
the union of yourself and the personality
who broke the even tenour of your ways

lightning juggled above the station portraying its grim battlements
thunder crashed upon the assembled people
she threw three flashes of self possessed rays
at him from her large radiant eyes
she ran to the drawer refusing the automobile
she snatched abruptly at the carrot
scenting with inexorable female intuition the precise positions
        afforded by reason of its pre-eminent significance
she ran from the room like a bitten wounded thing
and fell laughing upon the station master who had broken
the even
tenour of her ways

PHILIP O'CONNOR

Boston

I come from the city of Boston,
The home of the bean and the cod,
Where the Cabots speak only to Lowells,
And the Lowells speak only to God.

ANON.

BURLESQUE AND
PARODY

⌇

Imitation of Chaucer

Women ben full of Ragerie,
Yet swinken not sans secresie
Thilke Moral shall ye understand,
From Schoole-boy's Tale of fayre Irelond:
Which to the Fennes hath him betake,
To filch the gray Ducke fro the Lake.
Right then, there passen by the Way
His Aunt, and eke her Daughters tway.
Ducke in his Trowses hath he hent,
Not to be spied of Ladies gent.
'But ho! our Nephew,' (crieth one)
'Ho,' quoth another, 'Cozen John';
And stoppen, and laugh, and callen out, —
This sely Clerk full low doth lout:
They asken that, and talken this,
'Lo here is Coz, and here is Miss.'
But, as he glozeth with Speeches soote,
The Ducke sore tickleth his Erse-root:
Fore-piece and buttons all-to-brest,
Forth thrust a white neck, and red crest.
'Te-he,' cry'd Ladies; Clerke nought spake:
Miss star'd; and gray Ducke crieth Quake.
'O Moder, Moder' (quoth the daughter)
'Be thilke same thing Maids longen a'ter?
'Bette is to pyne on coals and chalke,
'Then trust on Mon, whose yerde can talke.'

ALEXANDER POPE

Fatal Constancy; or, Love in Tears

ACT III

The Palmy Grove

The Hero *solus*

Night, black-brow'd Night, queen of the ebon wand,
Now o'er the world has spread her solemn reign.
The glow-worm twinkles, and from every flower
The pearly dews return the pale reflex
Of CYNTHIA'S beams, each drop a little moon!
Hark! LINDAMIRA comes — no, 'twas the breath
Of Zephyr panting on the leafy spray.
Perhaps he lurks in yonder woodbine bower
To steal soft kisses from her lips, and catch
Ambrosial odours from her passing sighs.
O thief! —
    She comes; quick let us haste away.
The guards pursue us? heav'ns! — come then, my love,
Fly, fly this moment

> [Here a long conference upon love, virtue, the moon, etc., till
> the guards come up]

                — Dogs, will ye tear her from me?
Ye must not, shall not — O my heart-strings crack,
My head turns round, my starting eye-balls hang
Upon her parting steps — I can no more —
    So the first man from paradise exil'd
With fond reluctance leaves the blooming wild.
Around the birds in pleasing concert sing,
Beneath his feet th'unbidden flow'rets spring;
On verdant hills the flocks unnumber'd play,
Through verdant vales meand'ring rivers stray.

Blossoms and fruits at once the trees adorn,
Eternal roses bloom on every thorn,
And join POMONA's lap to AMALTHAEA's horn.

[Exeunt, torn off on different sides]

END OF THIRD ACT

ACT IV

A Prison

The Hero, in Chains

Ye deep dark dungeons, and hard prison walls,
Hard as my fate, and darksome as the grave
To which I hasten, wherefore do you bathe
Your rugged bosoms with unwholesome dews
That seem to weep in mockery of my woe?
– But see! some angel brightness breaks the gloom.
'Tis LINDAMIRA comes! So breaks the morn
On the reviving world. Thou faithful fair!

[Approaching to embrace her]

– Curse on my fetters, how they bind my limbs,
Nor will permit me take one chaste embrace.
Yet come, O come! –
                    What sayst thou? force thee to it!
Thy father force thee to OROSIUS' arms!
He cannot, will not, shall not – O my brain!
Darkness and devils! burst my bonds, ye powers,
That I may tear him piecemeal from the earth,
And scatter him to all the winds of heaven.
– What means that bell? – O 'tis the sound of death.
Alas, I had forgot I was to die!
Let me reflect on death, &c. –

                              But what is death,
Racks, tortures, burning pincers, floods of fire,
What are ye all to disappointed love?
Drag, drag me hence, ye ministers of Fate,
From the dire thought – OROSIUS must enjoy her!
Death's welcome now – OROSIUS must enjoy her!
Hang on her lips, pant on her breast! – O gods!
I see the lustful satyr grasp her charms,
I see him melting in her amorous arms.
Fiends seize me, furies lash me, vultures tear,
Hell, horror, madness, darkness and despair!

        [Runs off to execution]

        END OF FOURTH ACT

                    WILLIAM WHITEHEAD

            If You Have Seen

    Good reader! if you e'er have seen,
        When Phoebus hastens to his pillow,
    The mermaids, with their tresses green,
        Dancing upon the western billow:
    If you have seen, at twilight dim,
    When the lone spirit's vesper hymn
        Floats wild along the winding shore:
    If you have seen, through mist of eve,
    The fairy train their ringlets weave,
    Glancing along the spangled green; –
        If you have seen all this and more,
    God bless me! what a deal you've seen!

                        THOMAS MOORE

The Elderly Gentleman

By the side of a murmuring stream an elderly gentleman sat.
On the top of his head was a wig, and a-top of his wig was his hat.

The wind it blew high and blew strong, as the elderly gentleman
      sat;
And bore from his head in a trice, and plunged in the river his hat.

The gentleman then took his cane which lay by his side as he sat;
And he dropped in the river his wig, in attempting to get out his
      hat.

His breast it grew cold with despair, and full in his eye madness sat;
So he flung in the river his cane to swim with his wig, and his hat.

Cool reflexion at last came across while this elderly gentleman sat;
So he thought he would follow the stream and look for his cane,
      wig, and hat.

His head being thicker than common, o'er-balanced the rest of his
      fat;
And in plumped this son of a woman to follow his wig, cane, and
      hat.

GEORGE CANNING

On Captain Francis Grose, the celebrated Antiquarian

The Devil got notice that Grose was a-dying,
So whip! at the summons old Satan came flying;
But when he approach'd where poor Francis lay moaning,
And saw each bed-post with its burden a-groaning,
Astonish'd, confounded, cried Satan, 'By –
I'll want 'im, ere I take such a damnable load!

ROBERT BURNS

Crabbe-wise

John Richard William Alexander Dwyer
Was footman to Justinian Stubbs Esquire;
But when John Dwyer 'listed in the Blues,
Emanuel Jennings polish'd Stubbs's shoes.
Emanuel Jennings brought his youngest boy
Up as a corn-cutter – a safe employ;
In Holywell Street, St Pancras, he was bred
(At number twenty-seven, it is said),
Facing the pump, and near the Granby's head:
He would have bound him to some shop in town,
But with a premium he could not come down.
Pat was the urchin's name -- a red hair'd youth,
Fonder of purl and skittle-grounds than truth.

JAMES SMITH

On Grizel Grim

Here lies with Death auld Grizel Grim,
    Lincluden's ugly witch;
O Death! how horrid is thy taste
    To lie with such a bitch!

ROBERT BURNS

On a Schoolmaster in Cleish Parish, Fifeshire

Here lie Willie Michie's banes,
    O Satan! when ye tak him,
Gie him the schoolin' o' your weans;
    For clever deils he'll mak 'em!

ROBERT BURNS

Saragossa

(IN IMITATION OF THOMAS MOORE)

Pepita, my paragon, bright star of Arragon;
  Listen, dear, listen; your Cristobal sings.
From my cot that lies buried a short way from Lerida
  Love and a diligence lent me their wings.
Swift as a falcon I flew to thy balcony.
  (Is it bronchitis? I can't sing a bar.)
Greet not with merriment Love's first experiment;
  Listen, Pepita! I've brought my catarrh.

Manuel, the matador may, like a flat, adore
  Donna Dolores: I pity his choice,
For they say that her governor lets neither lover nor
  Anyone else hear the sound of her voice.
Brother Bartolomé (stoutish Apollo) may
  Sigh for Sabina – you'll pardon this cough? –
And Isabel's votary, Nunez the notary,
  Vainly – (that sneeze again? Loved one, I'm Off!)

H. S. LEIGH

'Twas Ever Thus

I never rear'd a young gazelle,
  (Because, you see, I never tried);
But had it known and loved me well,
  No doubt the creature would have died.
My rich and aged Uncle John
  Has known me long and loves me well,
But still persists in living on –
  I would he were a young gazelle.

I never loved a tree or flower;
   But, if I had, I beg to say
The blight, the wind, the sun, or shower
   Would soon have withered it away.
I've dearly loved my Uncle John,
   From childhood to the present hour,
And yet he will go living on –
   I would he were a tree or flower!

H. S. LEIGH

Only Seven

A PASTORAL STORY AFTER WORDSWORTH

I marvell'd why a simple child,
   That lightly draws its breath,
Should utter groans so very wild
   And look as pale as Death.

Adopting a parental tone,
   I ask'd her why she cried;
The damsel answered with a groan,
   'I've got a pain inside!

'I thought it would have sent me mad
   Last night about eleven.'
Said I, 'What is it makes you bad?
How many apples have you had?'
   She answered, 'Only seven!'

'And are you sure you took no more,
   My little maid?' quoth I;
'Oh, please, sir, mother gave me four,
   But they were in a pie!'

'If that's the case,' I stammer'd out,
    'Of course you've had eleven.'
The maiden answer'd with a pout,
    'I ain't had more nor seven!'

I wonder'd hugely what she meant,
    And said, 'I'm bad at riddles;
But I know where little girls are sent
    For telling taradiddles.

'Now, if you won't reform,' said I,
    'You'll never go to Heaven.'
But all in vain; each time I try,
That little idiot makes reply,
    'I ain't had more nor seven!'

POSTSCRIPT

To borrow Wordsworth's name was wrong,
    Or slightly misapplied;
And so I'd better call my song,
    'Lines after Ache-Inside.'

H. S. LEIGH

The Prater
•
AN EPIGRAM

LYSANDER talks extremely well:
On any subject let him dwell,
    His tropes and figures will content Ye:
He should possess to all degrees
The art of talk, he practises
    Full fourteen hours in four and twenty.

MATTHEW PRIOR

In Memoriam Technicam

I count it true which sages teach –
  That passion sways not with repose,
  That love, confounding these with those,
Is ever welding each with each.

And so when time has ebbed away,
  Like childish wreaths too lightly held,
  The song of immemorial eld
Shall moan about the belted bay.

Where slant Orion slopes his star,
  To swelter in the rolling seas,
  Till slowly widening by degrees
The grey climbs upward from afar.

And golden youth and passion stray
  Along the ridges of the strand, –
  Not far apart, but hand in hand, –
With all the darkness danced away!

THOMAS HOOD, JR.

The Old Man from Dunoon

There was an old man from Dunoon,
Who always ate soup with a fork,
  For he said, 'As I eat
  Neither fish, fowl nor flesh,
I should finish my dinner too quick.'

ANON.

Ballad

I

The auld wife sat at her ivied door,
    (*Butter and eggs and a pound of cheese*)
A thing she had frequently done before;
    And her spectacles lay on her apron'd knees.

The piper he piped on the hill-top high,
    (*Butter and eggs and a pound of cheese*)
Till the cow said 'I die', and the goose ask'd 'Why?'
    And the dog said nothing, but search'd for fleas.

The farmer he strode through the square farmyard;
    (*Butter and eggs and a pound of cheese*)
His last brew of ale was a trifle hard –
    The connexion of which with the plot one sees.

The farmer's daughter hath frank blue eyes;
    (*Butter and eggs and a pound of cheese*)
She hears the rooks caw in the windy skies,
    As she sits at her lattice and shells her peas.

The farmer's daughter hath ripe red lips;
    (*Butter and eggs and a pound of cheese*)
If you try to approach her, away she skips
    Over tables and chairs with apparent ease.

The farmer's daughter hath soft brown hair
    (*Butter and eggs and a pound of cheese*)
And I met with a ballad, I can't say where,
    Which wholly consisted of lines like these.

2

She sat with her hands 'neath her dimpled cheeks
    (*Butter and eggs and a pound of cheese*)
And spake not a word. While a lady speaks
    There is hope, but she didn't even sneeze.

She sat, with her hands 'neath her crimson cheeks;
    (*Butter and eggs and a pound of cheese*)
She gave up mending her father's breeks,
    And let the cat roll in her new chemise.

She sat, with her hands 'neath her burning cheeks,
    (*Butter and eggs and a pound of cheese*)
And gazed at the piper for thirteen weeks;
    Then she follow'd him out o'er the misty leas.

Her sheep follow'd her, as their tails did them.
    (*Butter and eggs and a pound of cheese*)
And this song is consider'd a perfect gem,
    And as to the meaning, it's what you please.

C. S. CALVERLEY

On a Lady's Sporting a Somerset

    I saw, I saw, I know not what,
    I saw a dash above a dot,
    Presenting to my contemplation
    A perfect mark of admiration!

L. STERNE (?)

Father William

'You are old, Father William,' the young man said,
  'And your hair has become very white;
And yet you incessantly stand on your head –
  Do you think, at your age, it is right?'

'In my youth,' Father William replied to his son,
  'I feared it might injure the brain;
But, now that I'm perfectly sure I have none,
  Why, I do it again and again.'

'You are old,' said the youth, 'as I mentioned before,
  And have grown most uncommonly fat;
Yet you turned a back-somersault in at the door –
  Pray, what is the reason of that?'

'In my youth,' said the sage, as he shook his gray locks,
  'I kept all my limbs very supple
By the use of this ointment – one shilling the box –
  Allow me to sell you a couple?'

'You are old,' said the youth, 'and your jaws are too weak
  For anything tougher than suet;
Yet you finished the goose, with the bones and the beak –
  Pray, how did you manage to do it?'

'In my youth,' said his father, 'I took to the law,
  And argued each case with my wife;
And the muscular strength, which it gave to my jaw,
  Has lasted the rest of my life.'

'You are old,' said the youth, 'one would hardly suppose
  That your eye was as steady as ever;

Yet you balanced an eel on the end of your nose –
    What made you so awfully clever?'

'I have answered three questions, and that is enough,'
    Said his father; 'don't give yourself airs!
Do you think I can listen all day to such stuff?
    Be off, or I'll kick you downstairs!'

LEWIS CARROLL

To R. K. (*1891*)

As long as I dwell on some stupendous
And tremendous (Heaven defend us!)
Monstr'-inform'-ingens-horrendous
Demoniaco-seraphic
Penman's latest piece of graphic.

BROWNING

Will there never come a season
Which shall rid us from the curse
Of a prose that knows no reason
And an unmelodious verse:
When the world shall cease to wonder
At the genius of an Ass,
And a boy's eccentric blunder
Shall not bring success to pass;

When mankind shall be delivered
From the clash of magazines,
And the inkstands shall be shivered
Into countless smithereens:
When there stands a muzzled stripling,
Mute, beside a muzzled bore:
When the Rudyards cease from Kipling
And the Haggards Ride no more?

J. K. STEPHEN

Sincere Flattery of R. B.

Birthdays? yes in a general way;
For the most if not for the best of men:
You were born (I suppose) on a certain day:
So was I: or perhaps in the night: what then?

Only this: or at least, if more,
You must know, not think it, and learn, not speak:
There is truth to be found on the unknown shore,
And many will find where few will seek.

For many are called and few are chosen,
And the few grow many as ages lapse:
But when will the many grow few: what dozen
Is fused into one by Time's hammer-taps?

A bare brown stone in a babbling brook: –
It was wanton to hurl it there, you say:
And the moss, which clung in the sheltered nook
(Yet the stream runs cooler), is washed away.

That begs the question: many a prater
Thinks such a suggestion a sound 'stop thief!'
Which, may I ask, do you think the greater,
Sergeant-at-arms or a Robber Chief?

And if it were not so? Still you doubt?
Ah! Yours is a birthday indeed if so.
That were something to write a poem about,
If one thought a little. I only know

P. S.

There's a Me Society down at Cambridge,
Where my works, *cum notis variorum*,

Are talked about; Well, I require the same bridge
That Euclid took toll of as *Asinorum*.

And, as they have got through several ditties
I thought were as stiff as a brick-built wall,
I've composed the above, and a stiff one *it* is,
A bridge to stop asses at, once for all.

J. K. STEPHEN

Sincere Flattery

OF W. W. (AMERICANUS)

The clear cool note of the cuckoo which has ousted the legitimate
  nest-holder,
The whistle of the railway guard dispatching the train to the
  inevitable collision.
The maiden's monosyllabic reply to a polysyllabic proposal,
The fundamental note of the last trump, which is presumably D
  natural;
All of these are sounds to rejoice in, yea, to let your very ribs
  re-echo with:
But better than all of them is the absolutely last chord of the
  apparently inexhaustible pianoforte player.

J. K. STEPHEN

On the College of Wadham at Oxford being insured from Fire, after a Member had been suspected of an unnatural Crime

Well did the amorous sons of Wadham
  Their house secure from future flame;
They knew their crime, the crime of Sodom,
  And judg'd their punishment the same.

ANON.

The Baby in the House

BY POVENTRY CATMORE

The Doctor

'A finer than your newborn child,'
  The Doctor said, 'I never saw,'
And I, but half believing, smiled
  To think he thought me jolly raw.
And then I viewed the crimson thing,
  And listened to its doleful squeal,
And rather wished the nurse would bring
  The pap-boat with its earliest meal.
My wife remarked, 'I fear, a snub,'
  The Doctor, 'Madam, never fear,
'Tis hard, Ma'am, in so young a cub
  To say.' Then Nurse, 'A cub! a Dear!'

The Godmother

'We ought to ask your sister Kate,'
  'Indeed I shan't,' Jemima cried,
'She's given herself such airs of late,
  I'm out of patience with her pride.
Proud that her squinting husband (Sam,
  You know I hate that little sneak)
Has got a post at Amsterdam,
  Where luckily he goes next week.
No, never ask of kin and kith,
  We'll have that wife of George Bethune's,
Her husband is a silver-smith,
  And she'll be sure to give some spoons.'

SHIRLEY BROOKS

A 'Prize' Poem

Full many a gem of purest ray serene,
That to be hated needs but to be seen,
Invites my lays; be present sylvan maids,
And graceful deer reposing in the shades.

I am the Morning and the Evening Star,
Drag the slow barge, or wheel the rapid car
While wrapped in fire the realms of ether glow,
Or private dirt in public virtue throw.

How small of all that human hearts endure
The short and simple annals of the poor!
I would commend their bodies to the rack;
At least we'll die with harness on our back!

Remote, unfriended, melancholy, slow,
Virtue alone is happiness below!
As vipers sting, though dead, by some review;
And now thou seest my soul's angelic hue.

SHIRLEY BROOKS

Poem by a Perfectly Furious Academician

I takes and paints,
Hears no complaints,
And sells before I'm dry;
Till savage Ruskin
He sticks his tusk in,
Then nobody will buy.

SHIRLEY BROOKS

Salad

O cool in the summer is salad,
  And warm in the winter is love;
And a poet shall sing you a ballad
  Delicious thereon and thereof.
A singer am I, if no sinner,
  My muse has a marvellous wing,
And I willingly worship at dinner
        The Sirens of Spring.

Take endive — like love it is bitter,
  Take beet — for like love it is red:
Crisp leaf of the lettuce shall glitter,
  And cress from the rivulet's bed:
Anchovies, foam-born, like the lady
  Whose beauty has maddened this bard;
And olives, from groves that are shady;
        And eggs — boil 'em hard.

MORTIMER COLLINS

King Arthur Growing Very Tired Indeed

King Arthur, growing very tired indeed
Of wild Tintagel, now that Lancelot
Had gone to Jersey or to Jericho,
And there was nobody to make a rhyme,
And Cornish girls were christened Jennifer,
And the Round Table had grown rickety,
Said unto Merlin (who had been asleep
For a few centuries in Broceliande,
But woke, and had a bath, and felt refreshed):
'What shall I do to pull myself together?'

Quoth Merlin, 'Salad is the very thing,
And you can get it at the "Cheshire Cheese".'
King Arthur went there: verily, I believe
That he has dined there every day since then.
Have you not marked the portly gentleman
In his cool corner, with his plate of greens?
The great knight Lancelot prefers the 'Cock',
Where port is excellent (in pints), and waiters
Are portlier than kings, and steaks are tender,
And poets have been known to meditate . . .
Ox-fed orating ominous octastichs.

MORTIMER COLLINS

Epitaph on a Taylor's Wife

Here lies a TAYLOR'S Counter-part,
Who lov'd a YARD with all her Heart.
Her cross-legg's spouse knew what would ease her,
And often stole a YARD to please her;
Yet all his CABBAGE would not save
The loving Baggage from the Grave:
But here she Slumbers, soon forgotten,
Now dead, not valued of a BUTTON.

ANON.

On Elphinstone's Translation of Martial's Epigrams

O thou whom Poetry abhors,
Whom prose has turned out of doors!
Heard'st thou that groan – proceed no further,
'Twas laurell'd Martial roaring murder.

ROBERT BURNS

After Dilettante Concetti

'Why do you wear your hair like a man,
      Sister Helen?
This week is the third since you began.'
'I'm writing a ballad; be still if you can,
      Little brother.
      (O Mother Carey, mother!
What chickens are these between sea and heaven?)'

'But why does your figure appear so lean,
      Sister Helen?
And why do you dress in sage, sage green?'
'Children should never be heard, if seen,
      Little brother.
      (O Mother Carey, mother!
What fowls are a-wing in the stormy heaven!)'

'But why is your face so yellowy white,
      Sister Helen?
And why are your skirts so funnily tight?'
'Be quiet, you torment, or how can I write,
      Little Brother?
      (O Mother Carey, mother!
How gathers thy train to the sea from the heaven!)'

'And who's Mother Carey, and what is her train,
      Sister Helen?
And why do you call her again and again?'
'You troublesome boy, why that's the refrain,
      Little brother.
      (O Mother Carey, mother!
What work is toward in the startled heaven?)'

'And what's a refrain? What a curious word,
          Sister Helen!
Is the ballad you're writing about a sea-bird?'
'Not at all; why should it be? Don't be absurd,
          Little Brother.
          (*O Mother Carey, mother!*
Thy brood flies lower as lowers the heaven.)'

          (A big brother speaketh:)

'The refrain you've studied a meaning had,
          Sister Helen!
It gave strange force to a weird ballad,
But refrains have become a ridiculous "fad",
          Little brother.
          And *Mother Carey, mother,*
Has a bearing on nothing in earth or heaven.

'But the finical fashion has had its day,
          Sister Helen.
And let's try in the style of a different lay
To bid it adieu in poetical way,
          Little brother.
          So, Mother Carey, mother!
Collect your chickens and go to – heaven.'

          (A pause. Then the big brother singeth, accompanying
          himself in a plaintive wise on the triangle:)

'Look in my face. My name · Used-to-was,
     I am also called Played-out and Done-to-death,
     And It-will-wash-no-more. Awakeneth
Slowly, but sure awakening it has,
     The common-sense of man; and I, alas!
          The ballad-burden trick, now known too well,
          Am turned to scorn, and grown contemptible –
A too transparent artifice to pass.

'What a cheap dodge I am! The cats who dart
   Tin-kettled through the streets in wild surprise
   Assail judicious ears not otherwise;
And yet no critics praise the urchin's "art",
Who to the wretched creature's caudal part,
   Its foolish empty-jingling "burden" ties.'

H. O. TRAILL

Rondel

Behold the works of William Morris,
   Epics, and here and there wall-papery,
   Mild, mooney, melancholy vapoury
A sort of Chaucer *minus* Horace.

Spun out like those of William Loris,
   Who wrote of amorous red-tapery,
Behold the works of William Morris,
   Epics, and here and there wall-papery!

Long ladies, knights, and earles and choris-
   ters in the most appropriate drapery,
   Samite and silk and spotless napery,
Sunflowers and apple blossoms and orris,
Behold the works of William Morris!

ANON.

On a General Election

The accursed power which stands on Privilege
(And goes with Women, and Champagne and Bridge)
Broke – and Democracy resumed her reign:
(Which goes with Bridge, and Women and Champagne).

HILAIRE BELLOC

The Higher Pantheism in a Nutshell

One, who is not, we see; but one, whom we see not, is;
Surely, this is not that; but that is assuredly this.

What, and wherefore, and whence: for under is over and under;
If thunder could be without lightning, lightning could be without
      thunder.

Doubt is faith in the main; but faith, on the whole, is doubt;
We cannot believe by proof; but could we believe without?

Why, and whither, and how? for barley and rye are not clover;
Neither are straight lines curves; yet over is under and over.

One and two are not one; but one and nothing is two;
Truth can hardly be false, if falsehood cannot be true.

Parallels all things are; yet many of these are askew;
You are certainly I; but certainly I am not you.

One, whom we see not, is; and one, who is not, we see;
Fiddle, we know, is diddle; and diddle, we take it, is dee.

ALGERNON CHARLES SWINBURNE

The Pin

As Nature H — y's Clay was blending,
Uncertain what her work should end in,
Whether in female or in male,
A Pin dropped in, and turned the Scale.

ANON.

The Chemist to his Love

I love thee, Mary, and thou lovest me –
Our mutual flame is like th' affinity
That doth exist between two simple bodies:
I am Potassium to thine Oxygen.
'Tis little that the holy marriage vow
Shall shortly make us one. That unity
Is, after all, but metaphysical.
Oh, would that I, my Mary, were an acid,
A living acid; thou an alkali
Endow'd with human sense, that, brought together,
We both might coalesce into one salt,
One homogeneous crystal. Oh, that thou
Wert Carbon, and myself were Hydrogen;
We would unite to form olefiant gas,
Or common coal, or naphtha – would to heaven
That I were Phosphorus, and thou wert Lime!
And we of Lime composed a Phosphuret.
I'd be content to be Sulphuric Acid,
So that thou might be Soda. In that case
We should be Glauber's Salt. Wert thou Magnesia
Instead we'd form the salt that's named from Epsom.
Couldst thou Potassa be, I Aqua-fortis,
Our happy union should that compound form,
Nitrate of Potash – otherwise Saltpetre.
And thus our several natures sweetly blent,
We'd live and love together, until death
Should decompose the fleshly tertium quid,
Leaving our souls to all eternity
Amalgamated. Sweet, thy name is Briggs
And mine is Johnson. Wherefore should not we
Agree to form a Johnsonate of Briggs?

ANON.

A Strike among the Poets

In his chamber, weak and dying,
    While the Norman Baron lay,
Loud, without, his men were crying,
    'Shorter hours and better pay.'

Know you why the ploughman, fretting,
    Homeward plods his weary way
Ere his time? He's after getting
    Shorter hours and better pay.

See! the Hesperus is swinging
    Idle in the wintry bay,
And the skipper's daughter's singing,
    'Shorter hours and better pay.'

Where's the minstrel boy? I've found him
    Joining in the labour fray
With his placards slung around him,
    'Shorter hours and better pay.'

Oh, young Lochinvar is coming;
    Though his hair is getting grey,
Yet I'm glad to hear him humming,
    'Shorter hours and better pay.'

E'en the boy upon the burning
    Deck has got a word to say,
Something rather cross concerning
    Shorter hours and better pay.

Lives of great men all remind us
    We can make as much as they,

Work no more, until they find us
    Shorter hours and better pay.

Hail to thee, blithe spirit! (Shelley)
    Wilt thou be a blackleg? Nay.
Soaring, sing above the mêlée,
    'Shorter hours and better pay.'

ANON.

The Modern Hiawatha

When he killed the Mudjokivis,
Of the skin he made him mittens,
Made them with the fur side inside,
Made them with the skin side outside,
He, to get the warm side inside,
Put the inside skin side outside;
He, to get the cold side outside,
Put the warm side fur side inside.
That's why he put fur side inside,
Why he put the skin side outside,
Why he turned them inside outside.

ANON.

The Young Man of Montrose

There was a young man of Montrose
Who had pockets in none of his clothes.
    When asked by his lass
    Where he carried his brass
He said 'Darling, I pay through the nose.'

ARNOLD BENNETT

The Shropshire Lad's Cousin

(AN EVEN GLOOMIER FELLOW THAN HIS
CELEBRATED RELATIVE)

When I go to the circus,
My heart is full of woe,
For thinking of the people
Who used to see the show,
And now are laid below.

They stood beneath the tent-cloth,
And heard the lion roar;
They saw the striped hyena
Revolve upon the floor;
And now they are no more.

I think of all the corpses
Worm-eaten in the shade;
I cannot chew my peanuts
Or drink my lemonade:
Good God, I am afraid!

I see the grave-worms feeding
Upon the tigers' tails;
I see the people quiet
As prisoners in jails,
Because they're dead as nails.

Then what's the good of watching
The horses and trapeze,
The big show and the little,
And the menageries? -
We're all a lot of fleas.

SAMUEL HOFFENSTEIN

Mr Walter de la Mare Makes the
Little Ones Dizzy

Speckled with glints of star and moonshine,
The house is dark and still as stone,
And Fido sleeps in the dogwood kennel
With forelegs over his mutton bone.

Then out of the walnut wood, the squirrels
Peep, with their bushy tails upreared,
And the oak on the wood's-edge stretches his branches,
And combs with his roots his mossy beard.

Then ninnies and oafs and hook-nosed zanies,
And rabbits bred in the realm of Wales,
Dance and scream in the frosty starlight,
Swinging the squirrels by the tails.

Till out of the wood, Grandfather Nightmare
Rides in a chariot of Stilton cheese,
And eats the ninnies, the oafs and zanies,
The rabbits ,the oak and the walnut trees.

SAMUEL HOFFENSTEIN

Mr W. H. Davies Snares Nature in a
Few Felicitous Stanzas

As lightly the wet fields I walked
Three leagues from London's noisy crowd,
I saw two ducks and seven drakes
And heard a blackbird singing loud.

Two dozen cows, knee-deep in grass,
I saw, and twenty-seven goats,
And heard a hundred sparrows pour
Upon a bank ten thousand notes.

And, though I've seen the golden notes
That rich men pour in city banks,
And know the sparrow's note is 'cheep',
I lifted up my heart in thanks.

SAMUEL HOFFENSTEIN

A Description of Maidenhead

Have you not in a Chimney seen
A sullen faggot, wet and green,
How coyly it receives the heat
And at both ends does fume and sweat?

So fares it with the harmless Maid
When first upon her Back she's laid;
But the kind experienced Dame
Cracks, and rejoices in the Flame.

JOHN WILMOT, EARL OF ROCHESTER

On the Upright Judge, who condemned the Drapier's Printer

In church your grandsire cut his throat;
    To do the job too long he tarried:
He should have had my hearty vote
    To cut his throat before he married.

JONATHAN SWIFT

A Recent Discovery

(An old bass-viol was lately bought for a few shillings at a farm sale not a thousand miles from Mellstock. Pasted on the inside of it was the following poem in a well-known handwriting. w. p.)

A RIGHT-OF-WAY: 186—

Decades behind me
When courting took more time,
In Tuphampton ewe-leaze I mind me
Two trudging aforetime:
A botanist he, in quest of a sought-after fleabane,
Wheedling his leman with 'Do you love *me*, Jane?'

Yestreen with bowed back
(To hike now is irksome),
Hydroptic and sagging the cloud wrack,
I spied in the murk some
Wayfarer myopic Linnaeus-wise quizzing the quitches
And snooping at simples and worts in the ditches.

Remarked he, 'A path here
I seek to discover,
A right-of-way bang through this garth here,
Where elsewhiles a lover
I prinked with a pocket herbarium, necked I and cuddled:
Now I'm all mud-sprent, bored and be-puddled.

'I'm long past my noon-time.
The Unweeting Planner
Again proffers bale for one's boon-time
By tossing a spanner
Or crowbar into the works without reckoning the cost, sir.
At eighty,' intoned he, 'life is a frost, sir.'

'When erst here I tarried
I knew not my steady
Had coolly, concurrently married
Three husbands already,
Not learnt I till later, what's more, that all three were brothers,
Though sprung they, it seems, of disparate mothers.

'Well, we two inspected
The flora of Wessex;
More specimens had we collected
Had she pandered less sex;
We botanized little that year . . . But I must be wending;
My analyst hints at amnesia impending.'

                                        WILLIAM PLOMER

I Wot What Not

Of all the dates I wis one wert
of all dates most unkind
Which wert the date comes up the street
With the date you leave behind

Of all the dukes to shake I wis
one wert no shakes to meet
Which wert I wot not how he stands
and wis not where his feet.

                                        EWART MILNE

Diamond cut Diamond

Two cats
One up a tree
One under the tree
The cat up a tree is he
The cat under the tree is she
The tree is wych elm, just incidentally.
He takes no notice of she, she takes no notice of he.
He stares at the woolly clouds passing, she stares at the tree.
There's been a lot written about cats, by Old Possum, Yeats, and Company,
But not Alfred de Musset or Lord Tennyson or Poe or anybody
Wrote about one cat under, and one cat up, a tree.
God knows why this should be left to me
Except I like cats as cats be
Especially one cat up
And one cat under
A wych elm
Tree.

EWART MILNE

Burlesque of Lope de Vega

If the man who turnips cries,
Cry not when his father dies,
'Tis a proof that he had rather
Have a turnip than his father.

Lines in Ridicule of Certain Poems Published in 1777

Wheresoe'er I turn my view,
All is strange, yet nothing new;
Endless labour all along,
Endless labour to be wrong;
Phrase that time hath flung away,
Uncouth words in disarray,
Trick'd in antique ruff and bonnet,
Ode and elegy and sonnet.

Imitation of the Style of . . .

Hermit hoar, in solemn cell
    Wearing out life's evening grey;
Strike thy bosom, Sage, and tell
    What is bliss, and which the way.

Thus I spoke, and speaking sigh'd,
    Scarce repress'd the starting tear,
When the hoary sage, reply'd,
    Come, my lad, and drink some beer.

SAMUEL JOHNSON

STREET CORNER SONGS

∽

The Ploughman's Wooing

Quoth John to Joan, wilt thou have me?
I Prithee now wilt, and Ise marry with thee:
My Cow, my Cow, my House and Rents,
And all my Lands and Tenements:
 Say my Joan, *say my* Joaney, will that not do?
 I cannot, cannot, come every day to woe.

I have Corn and Hay in the Barn hard by,
And three fat Hogs pend up in the sty;
I have a Mare and she's coal black:
I ride on her tail to save her back:
 Say my Joan, *say my* Joaney, will that not do?
 I cannot, cannot, come every day to woe.

I have a Cheese upon the shelf,
I cannot eat it all myself;
I have three good Marks that lie in a rag,
In the nook the Chimney instead of a bag:
 Say my Joan, *say my* Joaney, will that not do?
 I cannot, cannot, come every day to woe.

To marry I would have thy consent,
But faith I never could Complement;
I can say nought but hoy gee ho,
Terms that belong to Cart and Plough.
 Say my Joan, *say my* Joaney, will that not do?
 I cannot, cannot, come every day to woe.

ANON.

Unfortunate Miss Bailey

A captain bold from Halifax who dwelt in country quarters,
Betrayed a maid who hanged herself one morning in her Garters.
His wicked conscience smited him, he lost his Stomach daily,
And took to drinking Ratafia while thinking of Miss Bailey.

One night betimes he went to bed, for he had caught a Fever;
Says he, 'I am a handsome man, but I'm a gay Deceiver.'
His candle just at twelve o'clock began to burn quite palely,
A Ghost stepped up to his bedside and said 'Behold Miss Bailey!'

'Avaunt, Miss Bailey!' then he cries, 'your Face looks white and
    mealy.'
'Dear Captain Smith,' the ghost replied, 'you've used me
    ungenteelly;
The Crowner's 'Quest goes hard with me because I've acted
    frailly,
And Parson Biggs won't bury me though I am dead Miss Bailey.'

'Dear Corpse!' said he, 'since you and I accounts must once for all
    close,
There really is a one pound note in my regimental Small-clothes;
I'll bribe the sexton for your grave.' The ghost then vanished gaily
Crying, 'Bless you, Wicked Captain Smith, Remember poor Miss
    Bailey.'

ANON.

On Mr Churchill's Death

Prose-driving dunces, waddling fools in rhyme,
Scoundrels of ev'ry kind, by vengeance led,
Spit forth your venoms, poison all our clime,
Churchill, who scourged you to your holes, is dead.

J. C.

The Ratcatcher's Daughter

Not long ago in Vestminstier,
   There liv'd a ratcatcher's daughter –
But she didn't quite live in Vestminstier
   'Cause she lived t'other side of the water;
Her father caught rats, and she sold sprats,
   All round and about that quarter;
And the gentlefolks all took off their hats
   To the putty little ratcatcher's daughter.

She vore no 'at upon 'er 'ead,
   Nor cap nor dandy bonnet –
The 'air of 'er 'ead all 'ung down 'er back,
   Like a bunch of carrots upon it;
Ven she cried 'Sprats!' in Vestminstier,
   She had a sweet loud voice, sir,
You could hear her all down Parliament Street,
   As far as Charing Cross, sir.

Now rich and poor, both far and near,
   In matrimony sought her;
But at friends and foes she turn'd up her nose,
   Did the putty little ratcatcher's daughter.
For there was a man, sold lily-vite sand,
   In Cupid's net had caught her;
And right over head and ears in love
   Vent the putty little ratcatcher's daughter.

Now 'Lily-vite sand' so ran in 'er 'ead
   As she went along the Strand, oh!
She forgot as she'd got sprats on 'er 'ead,
   And cried, 'D'ye vant any lily-vite sand, oh!'
The folks amazed, all thought her crazed,
   As she went along the Strand, oh!

To see a gal with sprats on 'er 'ead
    Cry 'D'ye vant any lily-vite sand, oh!'

Now 'Ratcatcher's daughter' so ran in his head
    He couldn't tell vat he was arter,
So, instead of crying, 'D'ye vant any sand!'
    He cried, 'D'ye vant any ratcatcher's darter?'
His donkey cock'd his ears and laughed,
    And couldn't think vat he was arter,
Ven he heard his lily-vite sandman cry,
    'D'ye vant any ratcatcher's darter?'

They both agreed to married be
    Upon next Easter Sunday,
But Ratcatcher's daughter she had a dream
    That she wouldn't be alive on Monday; –
She vent vunce more to buy some sprats,
    And she tumbled into the vater,
And down to the bottom, all kiver'd up with mud,
    Vent the putty little ratcatcher's daughter.

Ven Lily-vite Sand 'e 'eard the news,
    His eyes ran down with water,
Said 'e, 'In love I'll constiant prove;
    And – blow me if I'll live long arter!'
So 'e cut 'is throat with a pane of glass,
    And stabb'd 'is donkey arter!
So 'ere is an end of Lily-vite Sand,
    Donkey, and the Ratcatcher's darter.

The neighbours all, both great and small,
    They flocked unto her berrein',
And vept that a gal who'd cried out sprats,
    Should be dead as any herrein.
The Corrioner's Inquest on her sot,
    At the sign of the Jack i' the Vater,

To find what made life's sand run out
    Of the putty little ratcatcher's daughter.

The werdict was that too much vet
    This poor young woman died on;
For she made an 'ole in the Riviere Thames,
    Vot the penny steamers ride on!
Twas a haccident they all agreed,
    And nuffink like self slaughter;
So not guilty o' fell in the sea
    They brought in the ratcatcher's daughter.

ANON.

On Mendax

MENDAX, 'tis said thou'rt such a liar grown,
That thou'st renounc'd all truth; and 'tis well done:
Lying best fits our manners, and our times;
But pr'ythee, Mendax, do not praise my rhimes.

ANON.

Epigram

INTENDED TO ALLAY PARTY SPIRIT

God bless the King, I mean the faith's defender;
God bless – no harm in blessing – the Pretender;
But who Pretender is, or who is King,
God bless us all – that's quite another thing.

JOHN BYROM

She was poor but she was honest

She was poor, but she was honest,
    Victim of the squire's whim:
First he loved her, then he left her,
    And she lost her honest name.

Then she ran away to London,
    For to hide her grief and shame;
There she met another squire,
    And she lost her name again.

See her riding in her carriage,
    In the Park and all so gay:
All the nibs and nobby persons
    Come to pass the time of day.

See the little old-world village
    Where her aged parents live,
Drinking the champagne she sends them;
    But they never can forgive.

In the rich man's arms she flutters,
    Like a bird with broken wing:
First he loved her, then he left her,
    And she hasn't got a ring.

See him in the splendid mansion,
    Entertaining with the best,
While the girl that he has ruined,
    Entertains a sordid guest.

See him in the House of Commons,
    Making laws to put down crime,

While the victim of his passions
  Trails her way through mud and slime.

Standing on the bridge at midnight,
  She says: 'Farewell, blighted Love.'
There's a scream, a splash – Good Heavens!
  What is she a-doing of?

Then they drag her from the river,
  Water from her clothes they wrang,
For they thought that she was drownded;
  But the corpse got up and sang:

'It's the same the whole world over,
  It's the poor that gets the blame,
It's the rich that gets the pleasure.
  Isn't it a blooming shame?'

ANON.

Death of my Aunt

My aunt she died a month ago,
  And left me all her riches,
A feather-bed and a wooden leg,
  And a pair of calico breeches;
A coffee-pot without a spout,
  A mug without a handle,
A baccy box without a lid,
  And half a farthing candle.

IRISH FOLK SONG

A Leary Mot

Rum old Mog was a leary flash mot,[1] and she was round and fat,
With twangs in her shoes, a wheelbarrow too, and an oilskin round
  her hat;
A blue bird's-eye o'er dairies fine – as she mizzled through Temple
  Bar,
Of vich side of the way, I cannot say, but she boned it from a Tar –

       Singing tol-lol-lol-lido.

Now Mog's flash com-pan-ion was a Chick-lane gill, and he
  gartered below his knee,
He had twice been pull'd,[2] and nearly lagg'd,[3] but got off by going
  to sea;
With his pipe and quid, and chaunting voice, 'Potatoes!' he would
  cry;
For he valued neither cove nor swell, for he had wedge[4] snug in his
  cly.[5]

       Singing tol-lol-lol-lido.

One night they went to a Cock-and-Hen Club at the sign of the
  Mare and Stallion,
But such a sight was never seen as Mog and her flash com-pan-ion;
Her covey was an am'rous blade, and he buss'd young Bet on the
  sly,
When Mog up with her daddle,[6] bang-up to the mark, and she
  black'd the Bunter's[7] eye.

       Singing tol-lol-lol-lido.

1. woman.	2. gaoled.	3. transported.	4. money.
5. pocket.	6. fist.	7. ragman.	

Now this brought on a general fight, Lord, what a gallows row –
With whacks and thumps throughout the night, till drunk as
     David's sow –
Milling up and down – with cut heads and lots of broken ribs,
But the lark being over – they ginned themselves at Jolly Tom
     Cribb's.
        Singing tol-lol-lol-lido.

ANON. *c.* 1811

On a Full-length Portrait of Beau Marsh

PLACED BETWEEN THE BUSTS OF
NEWTON AND POPE

Immortal Newton never spoke
    More truth than here you'll find;
Nor Pope himself e'er penned a joke
    More cruel on mankind.

The picture placed the busts between
    Gives satire all its strength;
Wisdom and wit are little seen –
    But folly at full length.

LORD CHESTERFIELD

A True Maid

No, no, for my Virginity,
    When I lose that, says ROSE, I'll dye:
Behind the Elmes, last Night, cry'd DICK,
    ROSE, were you not extremely Sick?

MATTHEW PRIOR

K 2

Under the Drooping Willow Tree

On a small six-acre farm dwelt John Grist the miller,
Near a pond not far beyond grew a drooping willow,
Underneath its spreading leaves sat Jane, his only daughter.
Meditating suicide in the muddy water.
Element Aqua Pura, Aqua Impura.
She sat by a duck pond of dark water,
Under the drooping willow tree.

She'd been jilted by a youth who had joined the Rifles,
A young man not worth a rap, who never stuck at trifles.
Though he promised to keep true, act like a faithful lover,
When his rifle suit he got, then leg bail he gave her,
Hooked it, stepped it, toddled, mizzled,
She sat by a duck pond of dark water,
Under the drooping willow tree.

'All alone I'm left,' says she, 'my poor heart is bursting;
Dearly did I love my Joe, though he wore plain fustian.
But my nose is out of joint, and don't it make me nettled.
In this pond I'll drown myself, then I shall be settled,
Bottled, finished, done for, flummoxed.'
She sat by a duck pond of dark water,
Under the drooping willow tree.

She'd no wish to spoil her clothes, so undressed that minute;
But the water felt so cold when her toes were in it.
'If it weren't so cold,' said she, 'I'd jump in like winking.'
Then she wiped her nose, and sat upon the edge thinking,
Pondering, puzzling, considering, ruminating.
She sat by a duck pond of dark water,
Under the drooping willow tree.

Like Venus she sat in her nude state staying;
Presently she was frightened by a donkey braying.
Like a frog she gave a leap, but worse luck she stumbled,
Lost her equilibrium, and in the water tumbled,
Fell in, pitched in, dropped in, popped in.
She fell in the duck pond of dark water,
Under the drooping willow tree.

When she found she'd fallen in, she then took to swooning;
Very long it would not have been, before she took to drowning.
But her Joseph was close by, saw her in the water,
With his crooked walking stick by the wool he caught her,
Nabbed her, grabbed her, seized her, collared her
From out of the duck pond of dark water,
Under the drooping willow tree.

He beheld her coming to with great acclamation,
And the tree bore witness to their reconciliation.
There it stands in all its pride, and will stand, moreover,
Unless the spot should be required by the London, Chatham and
      Dover
Railway Company, Limited, Good Dividends.
They'll sit by the duck pond of dark water,
Under the drooping willow tree.

ANON.

The Man in the Wilderness

The man in the wilderness asked of me,
How many strawberries grow in the sea?
I answered him as I thought good,
As many red herrings as grow in the wood.

ANON.

Bung your Eye

As a buxom young fellow was walking the street,
A certain fair maiden he chancèd to meet,
And as she drew near him she said, 'Will you buy?'
'Pray what do you sell?' She replies, 'Bung your eye.'

'To be serious, fair maiden, what have you got there?'
'Would you wish for an answer both kind and sincere?
''Tis Hollands Geneva, called by the bye,
As a nickname, my friend, it is Bung your eye.'

'If you be a gentleman, as you do appear,
To sell all my Geneva I need not to fear.
While I speak to some neighbours as they pass by,
So I'll leave you the care of this Bung your eye.'

The woman being gone it was his intent
To look into her basket he was fully bent,
In a few minutes after the young child did cry,
Instead of Geneva found a young Bung your eye.

'O curse this bad woman! What has she got here?
I have bought her Geneva, I vow, very dear,
I'm afraid all the lasses, as they pass me by,
Will call me the father of young Bung your eye.'

Bung your eye he took home, as I have heard say,
To have the child christen'd without more delay.
Says the parson, 'I'll christen the child by and bye,
What name will you give him?' He said 'Bung your eye.'

'Bung your eye,' said the parson, 'it is an odd name!'
'O yes, Sir,' he said, 'and an odd way it came,

I'm afraid all the lasses, as they pass me by,
Will think me the father of young Bung your eye.'

Come all you young fellows that walk in the street
Beware of those maidens you chance for to meet,
For Hollands Geneva put me in surprise,
Believe me, my girls, it bunged up both my eyes.

ANON.

$$L — y H — d W — e$$

In riches, titles, honours, see her soar;
In all the attitudes of grandeur – poor;
Her spare desert is of forbidden fruit;
Her pastry – lasting as a Chanc'ry suit.

ANON.

Epigram

WRITTEN SOON AFTER DR HILL'S FARCE CALLED
'THE ROUT' WAS ACTED

For physic and farces
His equal there scarce is;
His farces are physic,
His physic a farce is.

DAVID GARRICK

Epitaph on Lady Vane's Lap Dog Veny; At the Time of the Publication of her Memoirs, under the name of Lady Frail

At Thieves I bark'd, at lovers wagg'd my tail,
And thus I pleas'd both Lord and Lady Frail.

JOHN WILKES

Polly Perkins

I am a broken-hearted milkman, in grief I'm arrayed,
Through keeping of the company of a young servant maid,
Who lived on board and wages the house to keep clean
In a gentleman's family near Paddington Green.

> *Chorus:*
> She was as beautiful as a butterfly
> And as proud as a Queen
> Was pretty little Polly Perkins of
> Paddington Green.

She'd an ankle like an antelope and a step like a deer,
A voice like a blackbird, so mellow and clear,
Her hair hung in ringlets so beautiful and long,
I thought that she loved me but I found I was wrong.

When I'd rattle in a morning and cry 'milk below',
At the sound of my milk-cans her face she would show
With a smile upon her countenance and a laugh in her eye,
If I thought she'd have loved me, I'd have laid down to die.

When I asked her to marry me she said 'Oh! what stuff',
And told me to 'drop it, for she had quite enough
Of my nonsense' – at the same time I'd been very kind,
But to marry a milkman she didn't feel inclined.

'Oh, the man that has me must have silver and gold,
A chariot to ride in and be handsome and bold,
His hair must be curly as any watch spring,
And his whiskers as big as a brush for clothing.'

The words that she uttered went straight through my heart,
I sobbed and I sighed, and straight did depart;

With a tear on my eyelid as big as a bean,
Bidding good-bye to Polly and Paddington Green.

In six months she married, – this hard-hearted girl, –
But it was not a Wi-count, and it was not a Nearl,
It was not a 'Baronite', but a shade or two wuss,
It was a bow-legged conductor of a twopenny bus.

ANON.

On Joe

Joe hates a sycophant. It shows
Self love is not a fault of Joe's.

P. DODD

On the Collar of Tiger, Mrs Dingley's Lap-dog

Pray steal me not, I'm Mrs Dingley's
Whose heart in this four-footed thing lies.

JONATHAN SWIFT

A Note on the Latin Gerunds

When Dido found Aeneas would not come,
She mourned in silence, and was Di-do-dum.

RICHARD PORSON

On my Gude Auntie

Here lies my gude and gracious Auntie
Whom Death has packed in his portmanty.

ANON.

Darky Sunday School

Jonah was an immigrant, so runs the Bible tale,
    He took a steerage passage in a transatlantic whale;
Now, Jonah in the belly of the whale was quite compressed,
    So Jonah pressed the button, and the whale he did the rest.

Chorus:
        Young folks, old folks, everybody come,
        Join our darky Sunday School, and make yourself to hum.
        There's a place to check your chewing gum and razors at the
            door,
        And hear such Bible stories as you never heard before.

Adam was the first man that ever was invented.
    He lived all his life and he never was contented;
He was made out of mud in the days gone by
    And hung on the fence in the sun to get him dry.

The good book says Cain killed his brother Abel,
    He hit him on the head with a leg of a table.
Then along came Jonah in the belly of the whale,
    The first submarine boat that ever did sail.

Esau was a cowboy of the wild and woolly make,
    Half the farm belonged to him and half to Brother Jake;
Now, Esau thought his title to the farm was none too clear,
    So he sold it to his brother for a sandwich and a beer.

Noah was a mariner who sailed around the sea,
    With half a dozen wives and a big menagerie;
He failed the first season when it rained for forty days,
    For in that sort of weather no circus ever pays.

Elijah was a prophet who attended country fairs,
   He advertised his business with a pair of dancing bears;
He held a sale of prophecies most every afternoon,
   And went up in the evening in a painted fire balloon.

Then down came Peter, the Keeper of the Gates,
   He came down cheap on excursion rates.
Then along came Noah a-stumblin' in the dark,
   He found a hatchet and some nails and built himself an ark.

David was a shepherd and a scrappy little cuss,
   Along came Goliath, just a-spoilin' for a muss;
Now, David didn't want to fight, but thought he must or bust,
   So he cotched up a cobblestone and busted in his crust.

Ahab had a wife, and her name was Jezebel;
   She went out in the vineyard to hang the clothes and fell.
She's gone to the dogs, the people told the king,
   Ahab said he'd never heard of such an awful thing.

Samson was a strong man of the John L. Sullivan school,
   He slew ten thousand Philistines with the jawbone of a mule.
But Delilah captured him and filled him full of gin,
   Slashed off his hair and the coppers run him in.

Samson was a husky guy as everyone should know,
   He used to lift five hundred pounds as strong man in his show.
One week the bill was rotten, all the actors had a souse,
   But the strong-man act of Samson's, it just brought down the
      house.

Salome was a chorus girl who had a winning way,
   She was the star attraction in King Herod's Cabaret.
Although you can hardly say discretion was her rule,
   She's the favourite Bible figure in the Gertrude Hoffman school.

There are plenty of these Bible tales. I'll tell you one to-morrow
　　How Lot, his wife and family fled from Sodom and Gomorrah;
But his wife she turned to rubber and got stuck upon the spot,
　　And became a salty monument and missed a happy Lot.

Now Joey was unhappy in the bowels of the soil,
　　He lost his pretty rainbow coat because he wouldn't toil.
He hollered, howled, and bellowed until far into the night,
　　But of course you couldn't see him, for he was out of sight.

It happened that a caravan was passing by the place,
　　Laden down with frankincense and imitation lace.
They heard the Sheeney yelling and pulled him from the well,
　　If this ain't a proper ending, then you can go to Hell.

ANON.

Aunt Eliza

In the drinking well
　　Which the plumber built her,
Aunt Eliza fell –
　　We must buy a filter.

HARRY GRAHAM

The Firefly

The firefly's flame
Is something for which science has no name.
I can think of nothing eerier
Than flying around with an unidentified red glow on a person's
　　posterior.

OGDEN NASH

The Man on the Flying Trapeze

Oh, the girl that I loved she was handsome,
I tried all I knew her to please.
But I couldn't please her a quarter as well
As the man on the flying trapeze.

Chorus:

    Oh, he flies through the air with the greatest of ease,
    This daring young man on the flying trapeze.
    His figure is handsome, all girls he can please,
    And my love he purloined her away.

Last night as usual I went to her home.
There sat her old father and mother alone.
I asked for my love and they soon made it known
That she-e had flown away.

She packed up her box and eloped in the night,
To go-o with him at his ease.
He lowered her down from a four-story flight,
By means of his flying trapeze.

He took her to town and he dressed her in tights,
That he-e might live at his ease.
He ordered her up to the tent's awful height,
To appear on the flying trapeze.

Now she flies through the air with the greatest of ease,
This daring young girl on the flying trapeze.
Her figure is handsome, all men she can please,
And my love is purloinèd away.

Once I was happy, but now I'm forlorn,
Like an old coat that is tattered and torn,
Left to this wide world to fret and to mourn,
Betrayed by a maid in her teens.

ANON.

Roman Wall Blues

Over the heather the wet wind blows,
I've lice in my tunic and a cold in my nose.

The rain comes pattering out of the sky.
I'm a Wall soldier, I don't know why.

The mist creeps over the hard grey stone.
My girl's in Tungria; I sleep alone.

Aulus goes hanging around her place,
I don't like his manners, I don't like his face.

Piso's a Christian, he worships a fish;
There'd be no kissing if he had his wish.

She gave me a ring but I diced it away;
I want my girl and I want my pay.

When I'm a veteran with only one eye
I shall do nothing but look at the sky.

W. H. AUDEN

Charlie Piecan

It doesn't always do to let a mug know everything.
  Can't you rumble? I can.
  Look at Charlie Piecan.
He's a bloke as happy as the birds upon the wing.
  Charlie don't believe in
  Worrying and grieving.
He gave me half a quid a day or two ago, to back a horse.
  The gee-gee came in last of course.
He doesn't grumble but takes his beating like a don.
He little thinks that I forgot to put the money on.

Chorus:
  I haven't told him, not up to now,
  And if I did, most likely it would only cause a row.
  He doesn't know. I don't see any reason why he should.
  He wouldn't be any the happier if he did, so what's the good?

I used to think my sister would be left upon the shelf.
  So just as a finale,
  I hitched her on to Charlie.
I told him to look after her and keep her for himself.
  Nothing could be nicer;
  Charlie's going to splice her.
She's been and told him that she's only twenty-three. As I'm alive,
  She's getting on for forty-five.
And though he's always taking Liza for a walk,
He hasn't found that one of her legs is only made of cork.

Chorus:
  I haven't told him, not up to now,
  And if I did, most likely it would only cause a row.
  He doesn't know. I don't see any reason why he should.
  He wouldn't be any the happier if he did, so what's the good?

F. MURRAY and F. LEIGH

Wot Cher!

Last week down our alley came a toff,
Nice old geezer with a nasty cough,
Sees my Missus, takes 'is topper off
    In a very gentlemanly way!
'Ma'am,' says he, 'I 'ave some news to tell,
Your rich Uncle Tom of Camberwell
Popped off recent, which it ain't a sell,
    Leaving you 'is little Donkey Shay.

    'Wot cher!' all the neighbours cried,
        'Who're yer goin' to meet, Bill?
        Have yer bought the street, Bill?'
    Laugh! I thought I should 'ave died,
    Knocked 'em in the Old Kent Road!

Some says nasty things about the moke,
One cove thinks 'is leg is really broke,
That's 'is envy, cos we're carriage folk,
    Like the Toffs as rides in Rotten Row!
Straight! it woke the alley up a bit,
Thought our lodger would 'ave 'ad a fit,
When my missus, who's a real wit,
    Says, 'I 'ates a Bus, because it's low!'

    'Wot cher!' all the neighbours cried,
        'Who're yer goin' to meet, Bill?
        Have yer bought the street, Bill?'
    Laugh! I thought I should 'ave died,
    Knocked 'em in the Old Kent Road!

When we starts the blessed donkey stops,
He won't move, so out I quickly 'ops,
Pals start whackin' him when down he drops,
    Someone says he wasn't made to go.
Lor, it might have been a four-in-'and,
My Old Dutch knows 'ow to do the grand,
First she bows, and then she waves 'er 'and,
    Calling out we're goin' for a blow!

    'Wot cher!' all the neighbours cried,
      'Who're yer going to meet, Bill?
      Have yer bought the street, Bill?'
    Laugh! I thought I should 'ave died,
    Knocked 'em in the Old Kent Road!

Ev'ry evenin' on the stroke of five
Me and Missus takes a little drive,
You'd say, 'Wonderful they're still alive,'
    If you saw that little donkey go.
I soon showed him that 'e'd have to do
Just whatever he was wanted to,
Still I shan't forget that rowdy crew,
    'Ollerin', 'Woa! steady! Neddy woa!'

    'Wot cher!' all the neighbours cried,
      'Who're yer going to meet, Bill?
      Have yer bought the street, Bill?'
    Laugh! I thought I should 'ave died,
    Knocked 'em in the Old Kent Road!

ANON.

The Top of the Dixie Lid

Coolness under fire,
Coolness under fire.
Mentioned in despatches
For pinching the Company rations,
Coolness under fire.

Whiter than the whitewash on the wall,
Whiter than the whitewash on the wall.
Wash me in the water
Where you wash your dirty daughter
And I shall be whiter
Than the whitewash on the wall.

Now he's on the peg,
Now he's on the peg.
Mentioned in despatches
For drinking the Company rum.
Now he's on the peg.

Whiter than the top of the dixie-lid,
Whiter than the top of the dixie-lid.
Wash me in the water
Where you wash your dirty daughter
And I shall be whiter
Than the top of the dixie-lid.

ANON. (1914–18 War)

INDEX OF AUTHORS

INDEX OF FIRST LINES

*Some other Penguin
books are described on the
following pages*

MORE COMIC AND
CURIOUS VERSE

Edited by J. M. Cohen

More Comic and Curious Verse has been compiled on the
same principles as Mr Cohen's first *Comic and Curious* selec-
tion, though the net has been spread a little wider and the
number of unexpected catches is probably somewhat larger.
Among the haul are verses by the masters – Lear, Carroll,
Hood, Gilbert, and the rest – including the whole of 'The
Hunting of the Snark', as well as pieces by Victorians who
never aspired to any greater name than that of *Anon*. There
is also a fair representation of the living, including some
poems specially contributed to this book, and a number of
translations from the Austrian Christian Morgenstern, whose
vein of humour has long deserved naturalization. There is a
section of 'Tricks and Teases', which corresponds to nothing
in the previous volume, a nice bunch of parodies, a number
of 'Ballads to Harp Accompaniment', and a plentiful ration
of those short pieces that everyone likes to remember. As
before, magazines, periodicals, and old verse collections have
been combed for their occasional treasures, and proper attention has been paid to American versifiers, among them, of
course, Ogden Nash and other contributors to the *New
Yorker*, and also to those who appear in our own periodicals,
Punch in particular. D 31

THE PENGUIN SHAW

Bernard Shaw's *An Intelligent Woman's Guide to Socialism, Capitalism, Sovietism, and Fascism* was one of the first Pelican Books to be published in May 1937. Since then many of his plays have been published as Penguins. All of them are complete with Shaw's original prefaces, which put the argument of the play in strong and witty terms and serve as examples of Shaw's individual and assertive prose style. *The Black Girl in Search of God* also contains an essay on Christianity and the Bible, and thirteen other stories.

Androcles and the Lion – 566

The Apple Cart – 1169   *Back to Methuselah* – 200

The Black Girl in Search of God and Some Lesser Tales – 561

Major Barbara – 500   *Man and Superman* – 563

Plays Pleasant
(*Arms and the Man, The Man of Destiny, You Never Can Tell*) – 560

Plays Unpleasant
(*Widowers' Houses, The Philanderer, Mrs Warren's Profession*) – 561

Pygmalion – 300   *Saint Joan* – 565

Three Plays for Puritans
(*The Devil's Disciple, Caesar and Cleopatra, Captain Brassbound's Conversion*) – 562

The Doctor's Dilemma – 564